REVISE EDEXCEL
FUNCTIONAL SKILLS LEVEL 1

Information and Communication Technology

REVISION GUIDE

CW00740138

Series Consultant: Harry Smith

Author: Alison Trimble

TASK FILES
Some of the tasks in this book ask you to work with task files. Go to this webpage to download the task files:
www.pearsonschools.co.uk/ICTdownloads

A note from the publisher

In order to ensure that this resource offers high-quality support for the associated Pearson qualification, it has been through a review process by the awarding body. This process confirms that this resource fully covers the teaching and learning content of the specification or part of a specification at which it is aimed. It also confirms that it demonstrates an appropriate balance between the development of subject skills, knowledge and understanding, in addition to preparation for assessment.

Endorsement does not cover any guidance on assessment activities or processes (e.g. practice questions or advice on how to answer assessment questions), included in the resource nor does it prescribe any particular approach to the teaching or delivery of a related course.

While the publishers have made every attempt to ensure that advice on the qualification and its assessment is accurate, the official specification and associated assessment guidance materials are the only authoritative source of information and should always be referred to for definitive guidance.

Pearson examiners have not contributed to any sections in this resource relevant to examination papers for which they have responsibility.

Examiners will not use endorsed resources as a source of material for any assessment set by Pearson.

Endorsement of a resource does not mean that the resource is required to achieve this Pearson qualification, nor does it mean that it is the only suitable material available to support the qualification, and any resource lists produced by the awarding body shall include this and other appropriate resources.

THE REVISE SERIES
For the full range of Pearson revision titles, visit:
www.pearsonschools.co.uk/revise

Contents

1-to-1 page match with the Level 1 Revision Workbook ISBN 978 129214 587 1

A small bit of small print

Edexcel publishes Sample Assessment Material and the Specification on its website. This is the offi cial content and this book should be used in conjunction with it. The questions in Now try this have been written to help you practise every topic in the book. Remember: the real exam questions may not look like this.

Preparing for your test

The Level 1 Functional Skills ICT test will assess your ability to use a computer and software efficiently, safely and securely. Make sure you know what to expect in the test.

The tasks

The test is divided into two sections:

Section A

- **Task 1:** Use the internet to find and select information.

Section B

- **Task 2:** Process numerical data and produce graphs and charts.
- **Task 3:** Use the correct software to produce a document for a specific audience and purpose
- **Task 4:** Prepare an email with a message and an attachment.
- **Task 5:** Using ICT - managing your computer.

The files

You'll be given some computer files to work with, including:

- a folder of images
- a text file
- a spreadsheet
- a document called **ResponsesL1XXXXX**.

Evidence

The test paper will include some boxes with the heading **Evidence**. These boxes tell you how to present your answers. You might need to print out a document or a screen shot, or type something into the ResponsesL1XXXXX document. You should label any printouts clearly with your name, candidate number and centre number in the footer.

Screen shots

For some tasks, you'll need to take a **screen shot** (an image of your screen).

1 Press the 'Print Screen' key to save a screen shot to the Clipboard.

2 Open a Microsoft® Word document.

3 Right-click anywhere in the document and select 'Paste'.

4 Save the document with a sensible name.

Questions about using ICT

In the test you will be asked some general questions about ICT. You need to know about:

- staying safe online
- protecting data
- choosing appropriate software
- health and safety
- using ICT to work with others
- using system settings
- storing and backing up files.

Planning your time

Your test will last **2 hours**. There are **50 marks** available. You should spend:

- 15 minutes on **Section A**
- 1 hour and 45 minutes on **Section B**.

You might be asked to save your files to a new folder on your desktop rather than printing them out. Follow any instructions about file naming carefully.

Now try this

1 How many tasks should you complete in the test?

2 What information should you include on every printout?

Starting up and shutting down

Make sure you know how to **start up** and **shut down** your computer.

Starting up

To start up your computer, press the power button. Make sure the monitor (screen) is switched on too. You may need to log in before you can start using the computer.

User accounts

You won't need to be familiar with user accounts in the test but your computer at home, college or work may contain several user accounts. You can set up multiple user accounts on a computer. Each user can store his or her own files and applications. Before you shut down, check whether any other users are logged in, as they might need to save their work.

Logging in

If you have a login password, enter it carefully. Remember that passwords are **case sensitive** so you might need to use lower case and capital letters. If the password doesn't work, check that 'Caps Lock' isn't on.

Go to page 13 for more about choosing a secure password.

Shutting down

You need to know how to shut down a computer properly.

1. Click the Windows® icon.

2. Select 'Power'.

3. Choose 'Shut down'.

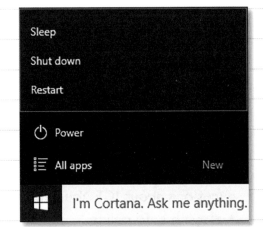

Before you shut down a computer, make sure you have saved any work that you have open. If you shut down without saving, your work might be lost.

Your computer might need to install updates before shutting down.

Golden rule

Make sure you shut the computer down properly rather than closing the laptop lid, pulling out the plug, or pressing the power button.

Now try this

1 What **two** things should you check before you shut down a computer?

2 You try to log into your user account but your password doesn't work. What could you check?

Hardware

You need to know what is meant by the term **hardware** and what you can use different types of hardware to do.

What is hardware?

Hardware is the word for the physical parts of a computer and other devices connected to it. Examples include:

- monitor
- keyboard
- mouse
- microphone
- tablet
- printer.

Solving hardware problems

There are some simple hardware problems you can solve yourself.

Make sure the device is plugged in and switched on.

Check for an error message on the device or on your screen.

Input and output devices

Input devices are items of hardware that **send** information to a computer.

Output devices **receive** data from a computer.

Some devices can be both. An ordinary monitor is an output device, whereas a touch **screen**, such as an interactive whiteboard, allows you to input instructions as well.

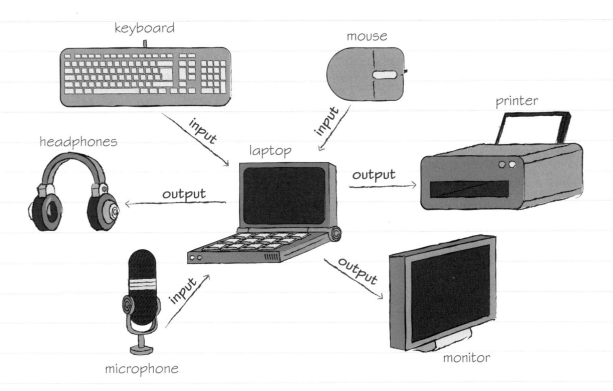

Now try this

List **two** items of hardware that are **both** input and output devices, and explain why they are both.

Software

Software is a general term for the applications and operating information, such as data and instructions, used by a computer. You can't see or touch software, but it makes your computer work.

Types of software

Computers use **two** types of software:

- applications
- operating systems.

Go to page 5 to read about using applications.

When applications stop working

Sometimes, your computer might freeze, or you might see a message that says an application has 'stopped responding' or 'encountered a problem'. If this happens during your test, put your hand up and tell an invigilator.

Which application?

An important part of your test is choosing the appropriate software to use for each task.

The task	Which application?
searching for information on the internet	a web browser such as Microsoft® Edge or Google Chrome™
preparing an email	email software such as Microsoft® Outlook
creating a document such as a poster, flyer, leaflet, information sheet or a letter	word processing software such as Microsoft® Word or publishing software such as Microsoft® Publisher
organising and analysing data, and producing a graph or chart	a spreadsheet application such as Microsoft® Excel
making a slide show presentation	presentation software such as Microsoft® PowerPoint

Now try this

Jamal is organising a fundraiser. His manager asks him to write a plan. Copy and complete Jamal's plan using these words and phrases.

PowerPoint	chart	presentation	word processing	Excel
web browser	Word	Chrome	spreadsheet	Outlook

To find the prices of items for the sweet stall, I'll open a _____ _____ , such as Microsoft® Edge and use a search engine. I will put the costs into a _____ using Microsoft®_____ and then make a pie _____ showing a breakdown of the costs. Next, I have to make a poster, so I'll use Microsoft® _____ which is a _____ _____ application. I will email the chart and the poster to my manager using Microsoft® _____. Finally, I will make a slideshow presentation for the next board meeting using Microsoft® _____.

Windows®

Windows® is an **operating system**, which is software that controls a computer's hardware and other applications. It acts as a **user interface**, letting you communicate with the computer, give it instructions and see the results.

The Windows® desktop

This guide uses Windows® 10. Some earlier versions of Windows® will look slightly different. You need to make sure you know where to find everything on your computer's desktop.

The Recycle Bin is where deleted files are stored.

Clicking the Windows® icon brings up the start menu.

The **search box** lets you search your computer for files or applications.

The **notification area** warns you if your computer is running slowly.

The **taskbar** displays icons for commonly used applications and any open windows.

Using apps

From your desktop, you can find the Windows® apps (applications) by clicking the Windows® icon in the bottom left corner.

The coloured tiles are the apps you use frequently.

Click 'All Apps', above the Windows® icon, to see a list of all the applications you have available.

To open an application, for example Microsoft® Word:

1 Scroll until you find Microsoft® Office.

2 Click on the arrow to bring up the list of applications available in this suite.

3 Click on Microsoft® Word.

The applications are listed in alphabetical order. Use the scroll bar to find the one you want.

Moving and resizing windows

You will find these buttons in the top right corner of any window you have open.

The **minus** button minimises the window but leaves it open.
You can restore it by clicking the application's icon on the taskbar.

The **rectangle** will make the window full screen. The **two rectangles** will make the window smaller again.

The **double-headed arrow** appears when you hover over the edge of a window. It allows you to manually resize a window to the size you want.

To move the window, click and hold the bar at the top of the frame and drag the window to where you want it.

The **cross** button closes the window.

Now try this

Use the search box to open the Calculator app. Minimise the window, restore it and then close it.

Problem solving

From time to time, you may experience problems when using your computer. Here are some potential solutions to help you if this happens.

Solving common problems

If something goes wrong in the test, don't panic! Look at the following common problems and their solutions.

I accidentally deleted some text.

Click the undo button to **undo** the last changes you made.

I deleted the wrong file.

Open the **Recycle Bin**. Right-click on the file and select 'Restore'.

I was working on a document in Microsoft® Word and my computer shut itself down before I could save it.

Microsoft® Word regularly **autosaves** and will offer to recover your file when you reopen the application.

Getting help in the test

You won't be allowed to ask for help with the tasks, or use the internet after Section A.

However, you can use Windows® Search and Microsoft® Office offline Help. To access this:

 Click the question mark icon at the top right of the window.

 Select the drop-down arrow and choose 'Word help from your computer'.

Getting it right

If something goes wrong with the computer during your test, you won't be expected to fix it. Raise your hand and let the invigilator know.

Don't waste too much time using help features during the test. Make sure you prepare well, so that you know what you need to do and where everything is.

Other ways to get help

When you are revising, you can use the online help in Microsoft® Office applications to learn how to do things.

You can also:

✓ Ask for help from your teacher or someone you know.

✓ Use a search engine, such as Google Web Search™, to find an answer to your questions.

Go to page 17 for more about search engines.

Now try this

Open Microsoft® Word and find the offline help. Find out how to change font colour (even if you already know!).

Health and safety

It is important to know how to minimise the risk of health problems associated with using computers. You also need to be aware of safety hazards and how to prevent accidents.

Are you sitting comfortably?

Your posture (the way you sit) is important. Poor posture can strain muscles and joints. Make sure your workstation is set up correctly.

Wear glasses if you are supposed to.

Make sure your elbows are at greater than 90° to the desk, and make sure your wrists are supported.

Sit with your back straight, lower back supported and shoulders relaxed.

Keep your feet flat on the floor or on a foot rest if they don't reach.

Adjust the brightness of your monitor to avoid eye strain.

Adjust the position of your monitor to avoid glare and reflections.

Make sure your eyes are level with the top of the monitor and about 50–80 cm away. Use a monitor stand if necessary.

Make sure there is no clutter under the desk and move any wires safely out of the way.

What else can you do?

- 👍 Tell your optician if you use computers a lot so they can test your eyes at the correct distance.
- 👍 Take regular breaks to avoid muscle strain and injuries such as Repetitive Strain Injury (RSI).
- 👍 Look away from the monitor frequently to avoid eye strain and headaches.
- 👍 Look out for hazards, such as trailing wires and plugs that could overheat.

What the law says

Under the Health and Safety at Work Act, an employer has to provide equipment that is safe and comfortable to use.

Golden rule

Never consume food and drink near a computer. Crumbs in the keyboard may require a costly repair, and a drink spilled on electrical equipment can put people's lives at risk.

Now try this

Your friend says she's heard that using computers can ruin your eyesight. What advice would you give her?

Settings and accessibility

Many of the settings on your computer can be changed to make it easier for you to use. Make sure you are able to use the test computer comfortably and with ease.

The Control Panel

You can change computer settings in the **Control Panel**. Type 'control Panel' into the Windows® Search box and select it on the results panel.

- Choose 'Mouse' to swap the buttons over if you are left-handed, or to change how quickly you need to double-click.
- Choose 'Display' to change the size of text and icons.
- Choose 'Speech Recognition' to use your voice to control the computer. This option can help someone who has impaired vision or who finds the keyboard hard to use.

Ease of Access Centre

The **Ease of Access Centre** brings together all the settings in the Control Panel that could help make the computer more accessible. Find it using Windows® Search or through the Control Panel. Make sure you know how to:

✓ use the Magnifier

✓ turn on Narrator that reads aloud the options in dialogue boxes

✓ change the colour and size of the mouse pointer

✓ choose a High Contrast theme.

Settings within applications

You can also make individual applications more accessible, too. Search 'accessibility' in the help feature of the application. In Microsoft® Office applications, you can customise the colour and size settings, and add keyboard shortcuts.

Golden rule

If you're using a shared computer, especially at work, check with the person responsible for IT before changing any settings to be sure that other people won't be affected.

Useful tips

- Use keyboard shortcuts if you struggle to use the mouse.
- Change the colour or size of the text to make it easier to read.
- Use the slider bar in Microsoft® Office applications to zoom in and out.

Now try this

1 Carla is left-handed and finds it difficult to click the left mouse button. What settings could she change to make it easier?

2 Jake is visually impaired and can't see the options in a window. Which features in the Ease of Access Centre could help?

Files and folders

Computer files should be organised within folders so they can be easily found. You need to know how to make new folders, as well as knowing how to move, copy and rename files and folders.

What is a file?

A **file** is a single 'package' of information. For example, a letter, song or video.

letter.docx

This letter would be a single file.

song.mp3

A music file may contain a single song or a whole concert. The filename may end in .mp3 or .wav.

image.jpg

An image filename might end in .bmp or .jpg.

What is a folder?

A **folder** is a container for one or more files that have something in common. You can use subfolders (folders within folders) to further organise files.

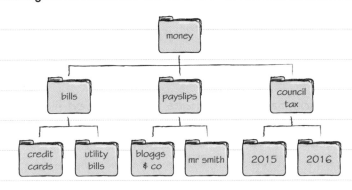

Protecting a file or folder

You can protect a file or folder by making it 'Read-only'.

1 Right-click the file or folder and select 'Properties'.

2 Tick the box with the label 'Read-only'.

3 Click the 'Apply' button'.

Alternatively, you can protect a document by giving it a password.

1 In Microsoft® Word go to 'File'. Click 'Protect Document' to view the drop-down menu.

2 Choose 'Encrypt with Password'.

3 Type a suitable password and select 'Ok'.

File and folder options

Right-clicking a file or folder brings up a menu.

- Choose 'Cut' to move the file or folder to a different location.
- Choose 'Copy' to copy the file or folder to the clipboard ready to paste in a different location.
- Choose 'Delete' to send the file or folder to the Recycle Bin.
- Choose 'Rename' to give the file or folder a new name.
- Choose 'Send to' to make a compressed (zipped) file or folder. Compressed files take up less storage space so they might be better for attaching to emails.

Think carefully before you delete anything. If you delete a file or folder on a USB stick, it won't be sent to the Recycle Bin, it will be permanently deleted.

Now try this

- Create a new folder on your Desktop called **Functional Skills**
- Open the folder **FilesPG9L1**
- Move the file **TestPG9L1** into the folder **Functional Skills**

Saving and printing

At the end of the test, you could be asked to save the files you have created and edited, or you could be asked to print them. If you're asked to print evidence of your work, check you know how to print from the computer you'll be using.

Saving files

 Click 'File' in the application you are using and choose 'Save As'.

 Select 'Computer' then double-click the folder where you want to save the file.

You should always save files regularly with a suitable name to avoid losing your work. Choose a name that reflects the content of the file. For example, you could call a poster about a party 'partyposter'.

Give the file a suitable name and click 'Save'.

If you make any changes to your saved file, click 'Save' at the top of the window to save a more recent version.

Naming files and folders

Make it easy to find the files and folders you need by choosing names that describe their contents. Here are some good and bad examples:

👍 2016 newsletters
👍 conference menu v1
👎 Joe 1
👎 Exam Task 3
👎 document1

Printing files

 Click 'File' in the application you are using.

 Click 'Print'.

 Choose the printer you want to use from the drop-down menu, then click 'Print'.

Printing tips

Before you press 'Print', look carefully at the print options and check the following:

- which printer you are using
- the number of copies
- which pages you are printing
- the page orientation and paper size.

If your printing doesn't come out, check the printer for an error message.

Now try this

- Create a new folder on your Desktop called **Spreadsheets**
- Open the file **TakingsPG10L1**
- Save a copy of the file into the folder **Spreadsheets**

Storing and backing up

You can save files and folders in many different places, including on removable storage devices and in 'the cloud'.

Removable storage

You can store your files on a computer itself or use a range of **removable storage devices**. The main types are:

- external hard drives
- CDs, DVDs and Blu-Ray Discs™
- USB memory sticks.

They can be used to **backup** important files, or **transport** files to another computer.

You can move files and folders to and from removable storage devices by using copy and paste or drag and drop.

Backing up

If you have important data on your computer, it is a good idea to store a copy in another place. There are lots of reasons to backup your files:

- your computer could be lost or stolen
- a virus might destroy or damage your files
- files could be deleted accidentally, or deliberately by hackers or malware
- your computer could develop a fault or be damaged.

Go to page 13 to read about keeping your files safe.

Zipping and unzipping

Zipping **compresses** a file or folder so that it takes up less storage space and can be sent and received faster.

You can attach a zipped folder to an email. (You can't attach a folder to an email.)

Creating a zipped folder

 Right-click a closed folder.

2 Choose 'Send to Compressed (zipped) folder'.

You'll see an identical folder with a zipper icon – the original is unaffected.

You can zip an individual file, too.

Unzipping

1 Right-click a zipped file or folder.

 Choose 'Extract All' and choose where you want to save the files

 Click 'Extract'.

Cloud storage

'**Cloud storage**' **services**, such as Dropbox™, allow you to store your files online. There are advantages and disadvantages associated with storing files in 'the cloud'.

- 👍 You can access your files from any device with internet access.
- 👍 It's easy to share files with others.
- 👍 You can easily work together on a document with other people.
- 👍 Your files are safe if something goes wrong with your computer or you lose your removable storage.
- 👎 You can't access your files while you're offline, unless you've saved them on your computer as well.

Now try this

You are planning to take your laptop to a conference. Your laptop contains all the files for your business plan.

1 Name **one** type of removable storage device you could use to backup your files.

2 Give **two** reasons why it is important to backup your files.

Screen shots

A screen shot is an image of what is on your screen. In the test, you could be asked to take a screen shot to show evidence of your work.

Taking a screen shot

To take a screen shot of your whole screen:

1 Press the 'Print screen' key on your keyboard. This saves an image of your screen on the **clipboard**.

2 In a Microsoft® Word document, right-click, and choose 'Paste'.

If your 'Print screen' key has more than one function, you may need to press another key at the same time. Make sure you know how to take a screen shot on the computer you'll be using in the test.

The Snipping Tool

If you only want to capture part of your screen, you can use the cropping tool in Microsoft® Word, or you can use the **Snipping Tool**.

You can find it by typing 'snipping tool' in the search box.

Snipping Tool   —   ☐   ✕

New ▾ Delay ▾ ✕ Cancel Options

Select a snip type from the menu or click the New button.

1 Choose 'Rectangular Snip' from the New drop-down menu.

2 Click in one corner of the screen and drag the cursor around the part of the screen you want to capture.

3 Paste the snip into your Microsoft® Word document.

Getting it right

Make sure screen shots include all relevant information, such as the key words in an internet search and the name of the search engine.

✓ Aim to fit no more than two screen shots on a page – you can crop and enlarge to show detail if necessary.

✓ Before taking a screen shot, make sure that you maximise the window to make it fill the screen.

✓ Zoom in if key information isn't visible.

Go to page 31 to revise using the cropping tool.

Now try this

Check that your screen shot includes all the information asked for in the question.

- Use a search engine to search the internet for the key words 'tourist attractions cheshire'.

- Take a screen shot of your whole screen and paste it into a blank Microsoft® Word document.

- Crop the screen shot to show only the top left quarter of the screen.

- Enlarge the cropped screen shot to fill half your A4 page.

- Save the file with a suitable name in a folder on your desktop.

Keeping your information safe

It is important to know how to keep files containing personal or business information safe. You need to know how to protect your computer from malware such as viruses and spyware.

Passwords

Passwords are a good way of keeping your information safe. You can use passwords to protect computers, files, removable storage devices and online accounts.

Never tell anyone your passwords and avoid writing them down anywhere.

Choosing a strong password

You should use strong passwords that are easy for you to remember, but difficult for others to guess. Choose something memorable to you and then change some of the letters and add numbers to make it harder to guess.

👍 If your favourite football team is Liverpool, you could try adding some capital letters and numbers: L1v3RpOOL

👍 If your grandma's name is Margaret, you could add the year of her birth and some capital letters: mAR45garet

Golden rule

A strong password should:

✓ contain a mixture of letters, numbers and symbols

✓ contain both capital and lower case letters

✓ be at least 8 characters in length.

✓ be memorable to you, but not easily guessed.

Stay secure by changing your passwords regularly.

Go to page 9 to read about protecting your documents.

Malware

Malware is short for 'malicious software'. It refers to software that installs on your computer without your knowledge and has a harmful effect. Malware can affect your computer in lots of ways.

* Viruses can slow down your computer, stop applications working, or even send emails from your account.

* Adware may load pop-up ads on your screen, or even replace your home page with adverts.

If you share files, send emails or are part of a network when you are infected, you could pass the malware on to others too.

Protecting against malware

* Install antivirus software, such as Norton AntiVirus™, or AVG AntiVirus™, and keep it up-to-date.

* Make sure your computer automatically installs Windows® Update.

* Don't download files from untrustworthy websites.

* Don't open attachments in suspicious emails.

Now try this

Think about which password is memorable and relevant, and difficult for others to guess.

Malcolm works in a nursery. Which of these would make the best password for the computer he uses there?

(a) nursery   (b) nUr5Ery£

(c) 12345678   (d) Malcolm

Putting it into practice

You will use skills covered in this chapter for every task in the test. The test paper may also include one or two specific questions about using ICT. When you answer this kind of question, make sure you do the following things.

✓ Read the question carefully.

✓ Look at how many marks are available and include the same number of points in your answers.

✓ Be specific.

✓ Check your answer.

1 Giovanni works for Bickleton PC Supplies and needs to choose a login password for the office computer. Which of these passwords should he choose? Give a reason for your choice.

 Make sure you give a reason for your choice. You should explain why the password you have chosen is the stronger of the two.

(a) Bickleton

(b) bickL3&tOn

(2 marks)

2 Give **two** ways you could reduce the risk of a virus harming your computer files.

 Be specific! It isn't enough to just say 'antivirus'. Make sure you give two different ways as there are two marks available.

(2 marks)

3 Name **two** input devices and **two** output devices.

 If you don't remember the meaning of these words' think about how they start with 'in' and 'out'.

(4 marks)

4 Identify **one** system setting that you could change to make a computer more accessible for a colleague with a visual impairment.

 You can look in the Ease of Access Centre, even in the test!

(1 mark)

5 Give **two** ways you could avoid health problems when using a computer for long periods of time.

  There are many possible answers to this question. You only need to think of two! Don't spend time thinking of more answers than you need.

(2 marks)

6 Give **two** reasons why you should backup your important files.

(2 marks)

The internet

You need to know the difference between the internet, the web and a web browser. You will need to use the internet to find and select information for Section A of the test.

What is the internet?

The **internet** is a network of computers and devices all over the world, connected by cables and wireless technology. A **website** is a set of files, called **webpages**, stored on **web servers** across the world.

You can access the internet using a **broadband** connection or mobile services, such as 4G.

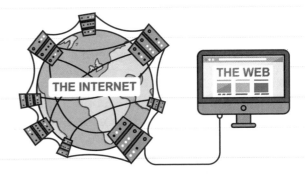

What can you use the internet for?

People use the internet every day at work and at home for many reasons, including:

- searching for information
- communicating via email or video calls
- playing games
- shopping
- listening to music
- watching TV or films.

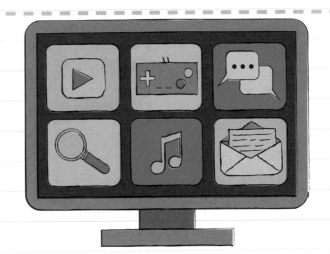

What is the web?

The **World Wide Web**, or '**the web**', is the name for a collection of **websites** that can be accessed via the internet.

Websites are made up of **webpages**. Each webpage has a unique web address. For example, www.pearson.com

> Go to page 16 for more about navigating a website.

What is a web browser?

To view web pages and move between them, you use software called a **web browser**. Examples include:

- Microsoft® Edge
- Google Chrome™
- Mozilla Firefox®
- Safari®.

You need to type a web address exactly, or the web browser won't be able to find it.

Now try this

1 Copy and complete the following paragraph using these words or phrases

| websites | internet | webpages | web |

The _____ is the name for a collection of _____ that can be accessed via the

_____ . Websites are made up of _____ .

2 What's wrong with this web address: wwwpearson.com?

Navigating a website

For Section A of the test, you need to know how to use the features of website to move around it and find information.

Navigating a website

Your web browser has many useful features to help you move around the internet.

Click this plus sign to open a new **tab**. Tabs allow you to keep one website open while you visit another in the same window.

Type a URL (web address) in the address bar. Web addresses begin **http://** or **https://** (secure sites). This is often (but not always) followed by **www**.

Use the **navigation arrows** to move forward and back through web pages you've visited. Use the **refresh arrow** to reload a page.

Type key words in the **search box** to find things quickly.

Click a **hyperlink** to go to another page. Text hyperlinks are often a different colour or underlined. Pictures can be hyperlinks too.

Microsoft® Edge

This guide uses Microsoft® Edge, which is the default web browser used by Windows® 10.

If you know the website you want to go to, type it in the address bar.

Alternatively, you can type key words into the address bar and the search engine, Microsoft® Bing, will search the web for relevant results. Most web browsers work in very similar way to Microsoft® Edge.

Hyperlinks

You can right-click or left-click hyperlinks.

- **Left-clicking** takes you to a new page.
- **Right-clicking** gives you two choices: open the new page in a new tab, or open the page in a new window.

Go to page 17 to revise internet searches.

Now try this

Using the web browser you will use in your test:

1 Open the website www.bbc.co.uk in one tab and www.nhs.uk in another tab.

2 Left-click a link of your choice on www.bbc.co.uk to open that page.

3 Right-click a link of your choice on www.nhs.uk to open it in a new window.

Searching for information

Task 1 in the test requires you to perform an internet search. You will have 15 minutes for this task. You might be asked to save some information to use later in the test.

What is a search engine?

Search engines search the web for information. The search results consist of links to different webpages that include the **search terms** you have typed in. Some examples of search engines are Yahoo® Search, Microsoft™ Bing and Google Web Search™.

Efficient searches

Choose efficient search terms to get the best results for your search. Follow these tips to improve the efficiency of your internet search.

- Use a few important words only.
- Don't worry about the order of your search terms.
- Don't worry about capital letters and punctuation.

Choosing the right search

Suppose you are planning a trip to Estrick Zoo and you want to know how early you could arrive. Instead of typing out this question, think about what the web page with the answer would say:

👎 *I'm going to Estrick Zoo how early can I get in?*

This search will bring up a lot of results and the opening hours page of Estrick Zoo's website is unlikely to be on the first page.

👍 *Estrick Zoo opening times*

This search will yield fewer results and the opening hours page is likely to be the first result.

Providing evidence

If you're asked to paste a screen shot of your search and the results into the 'Responses' document, the screen shot should show:

✓ the search engine you used
✓ the words you searched for
✓ the top of the list of results.

If you're asked for the address of the webpage where you found a piece of information, make sure you give the address of the webpage and not the address of the search engine results.

Make sure the keywords and name of the search engine are visible on your print-out.

  Estrick zoo opening times 🔍

All   Images   Videos   Shopping

Estrick Zoo

 www.estrickzoo.org
We're open every day from 9 a.m until 6 p.m. on weekdays and 10 a.m. until 4 p.m. at the weekend. Last entry is 1 hour before closing. The zoo is closed for Christmas Day and Boxing Day. Book your tickets now!

Local attractions - Estrick
www.visitestrick.com/things-to-do
Estrick Zoo is the number one zoo in the North. Open all year round. With 10,000 animals to see and 160 acres to explore, there's fun for all the family........

Voucher zone
www.voucherzone/localattractions
Our exclusive voucher gives you 40% off family tickets to Estrick Zoo. Go to the zoo website for details about opening times and directions. Cont act one of our customer service advisors for more information on the deal........

Now try this

- Use an internet search engine to find the name of the castle in the Ribble Valley in Lancashire and the postcode of its museum.
- Type your answers and paste a screen shot of your search and results in the file called **ResponsesPG17L1**
- Give the URL of the web page where you found the information.

Evaluating information

Information found on the internet can come from any source and may not always be reliable, unbiased, up-to-date or relevant. When searching in Task 1 of your test, you need to evaluate all of these things to decide whether information is fit-for-purpose.

Is the source reliable?

Anyone can create websites and publish information on the internet. In your test, you need to distinguish between reliable and unreliable sources. Who is the author?

- Is he/she an expert in the subject?
- Is he/she associated with a reputable, official organisation?
- Is there any contact information so you can ask about the sources used?
- What is his/her purpose?

The most reliable websites are usually set up by official organisations and companies. These websites can be identified by their web address.

Web addresses

You can often identify reliable webpages from their web address.

web address ending	source
.com	commercial organisations
.org	not-for-profit organisations
.co.uk	UK company's website
.gov	government organisation
.ac.uk or .sch.uk	universities, schools and colleges

Is the information up-to-date?

Information may have been reliable and accurate when written, but if it is not updated regularly it may become out-of-date:

- Look for a 'last updated' date.

Last updated: 25ᵗʰ August 2012

- Check whether the content refers to past dates as though they are in the future, e.g. 'We are planning a great event for August 2013.'
- Look for copyright information at the bottom of the page. There should be a year mentioned.

©2016. All rights reserved.

Is the source objective?

If the writer is giving you **facts**, or presenting both sides of a debate fairly, you may decide that they are **unbiased**. Alternatively, if they are trying to persuade you to do something or are just sharing their opinion, they may be **biased**.

Is the information relevant?

Make sure the information is relevant to the question you are being asked. Underline key words in the question to help you focus your search. For example, if you are asked to find a contact number, you shouldn't give an email address instead.

Now try this

You are thinking of having double-glazed windows fitted at your workshop and need some advice on which company to use to fit them. Which of these websites would you choose and why?

(a) the website of window-fitting company

(b) a website where people post reviews of double-glazing companies.

Staying legal

Many of the articles, images, audio and video files you can find on the internet are protected by copyright law. You don't need to be a legal expert but you do need to be aware of **copyright law** and **The Data Protection Act.**

Protecting information

1 **Copyright law** protects producers of written work, music, video, software and images. It is illegal to use copyrighted material without permission.

2 **The Data Protection Act** is a law which affects organisations that store personal information on a computer or in paper files. It states that personal data stored by organisations must be:

- necessary
- accurate and up-to-date
- stored safely, e.g. in locked filing cabinets or protected by a strong password
- available to the person on request.

What is protected by copyright?

© If you can't see a copyright symbol on something, it doesn't mean you are free to use it in your own publication. Always assume something is protected by copyright unless you can find evidence that it isn't. Copyright-free material includes material that is:

- in the **public domain**, which means you can use it freely.
- made available for reuse by the copyright owner, for example, using a Creative Commons (CC) license.

Plagiarism

Plagiarism is the act of taking someone else's work and pretending it is your own. Doing this is a breach of copyright law. Examples of plagiarism include:

- copying part of an article you find on the web and include it in a report you are writing
- using a photo on your blog that you've taken from another website and labelling it: 'Here's a photo I took yesterday.'

What can't you do with copyrighted material?

Copyright law prohibits you from doing the following with someone else's work:

- copying it
- distributing it
- displaying it
- modifying or adapting it.

Golden rule

If you are in doubt about whether something is protected by copyright, you should contact the owner or seek further advice.

Now try this

1 What does copyright law forbid you from doing?

2 Name one type of material that you can use freely.

Putting it into practice

In the test, you'll need to find and select accurate, relevant, unbiased information on the internet and provide evidence of your search. You could also be asked about how to reuse information legally, following copyright law and The Data Protection Act. Look at the following tasks to see what kind of things you could be asked in the test.

1 You **may** use the internet for this task only.

Julie works as a hotel receptionist and has been asked to create an information sheet about local events. She needs to find the name of the <u>Cheshire village</u> which has an <u>annual pie-rolling contest</u>, and the <u>month</u> it is held.

You can't go back on the internet when you've started the next task. Double-check that you've found all the information you need and make sure it is saved in your **Responses** document.

Use an internet search engine to find the name of the village and the month the contest is held.

Show how you did this by completing **ResponsesPG2OL1** with:

Underline the key words in the task so you know exactly what you are searching for.

- a screen shot of the search engine including the key words you typed in to find the website
- the name of the village and the month the contest is held
- the full web address (URL) that you used.

The web address you give must be for the website where you found the information, not for the search engine.

Evidence

A copy of the completed document **ResponsesPG2OL1** saved in a folder on your Desktop.

Resave **ResponsesPG2OL1** for use in Task 2.

Go to page 12 to revise how to take screen shots.

(4 marks)

2 Hatem, Julie's manager, asks her to double-check that everything on the information sheet is accurate.

Give **two** reasons why people should be careful about using information they find on the internet.

Notice that this question is worth 2 marks. A one-word answer would not be enough to gain both marks.

(2 marks)

What is email?

Email (electronic mail) is a method of sending messages and files via the internet between computers and other devices. For the test you need to know how to:

- prepare to send an email
- add attachments to an email.

Types of email

There are two main types of email:

1 An **email client** is an application that you install on your computer.
One example is Microsoft® Outlook, which comes as part of the Microsoft® Office package. You can use it offline to compose messages, and then send them later when you have a connection.

2 **Web-based email** services use the web, so they can only be accessed from computers with an internet connection. Examples include Gmail™, Microsoft™ Outlook.com and email accounts provided by internet service providers. There's no software to install as you send messages from a website using your web browser.

Email addresses

Both types of email give you your own email address, and a mailbox where you can store messages you receive and compose messages to send. Sometimes, in a business, more than one person may share an email address, such as customerservice@example.com.

Email addresses have three parts:

A unique ID such as the person's name. It could also be the name of a business or department, such as 'customerservice'.

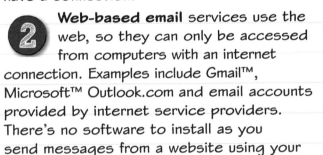

dev19@example.com

An **@ symbol**, so that the computer recognises it as an email address.

The **domain** where the email address is set up, usually ending in .com or .co.uk.

Advantages of email

- 👍 You can access a web-based account anywhere and on any device when you have access to the internet.
- 👍 Emails usually arrive in a few seconds and can be sent any time of day or night, so you never miss the post!
- 👍 There's no need to buy a stamp because most email accounts are free.
- 👍 You can keep a permanent record of what has been said, unlike a phone call.
- 👍 You can send an email to lots of people at the same time.
- 👍 You can attach documents to share with other people.

Disadvantages of email

- 👎 The recipient of an email needs access to the internet to receive it.
- 👎 An email sent to one person can be easily forwarded to many others, including people you wouldn't want to see it.
- 👎 Malware is easily transmitted via email.
- 👎 People can be deceived by phishing emails.
- 👎 You don't always know whether your email was received and read, unlike an answered phone call.

Go to page 22 to revise sending and receiving emails.

Now try this

Aoife needs to contact all her customers to cancel all her appointments for that day.
List **two** advantages and **two** disadvantages of using email instead of phone calls to let them know.

Sending and receiving emails

In the test, you'll be asked to prepare an email with an attachment. Even if you're confident sending and receiving emails, this page contains useful points for you to revise.

Creating an email

If you are using Microsoft® Outlook:

1 Click 'New Email' to start a new message.

2 In the test, you'll be given an email address to send your email to. This must be copied exactly into the 'To:' box.

3 You must add a relevant subject in the 'Subject:' box, stating what the email is about.

4 Attach the correct document.

5 Include a relevant message.

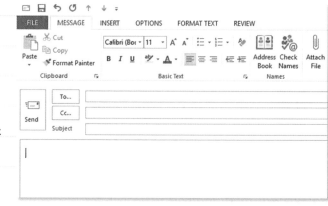

> Go to page 24 for more about email messages.

Getting it right

In the test, you won't actually send the email, but you will be asked to take a screen shot of it. Make sure everything listed above is visible.

Sending an email

Unlike in the test, if you were really sending the email, you would click the 'Send' icon to the left of your screen once you have completed the email.

- If you were online, it would go straightaway, and the recipient could see it in seconds.
- If you were offline, it would go into a temporary area, the 'Outbox', and be sent when you next go online.

Replying and forwarding

When you receive an email, you can respond in several ways.

- You can reply to the person who sent an email by clicking 'Reply'.
- You can reply to everyone an email was addressed to by clicking 'Reply All'.
- You can send an email to a person who didn't receive the original email, by clicking 'Forward'.

Now try this

Compose and send an email to your own email address with a suitable subject and message, attaching a file of your choice.

The email should appear in your 'Sent' folder **and** your 'Inbox', as you've sent it to yourself!

Email attachments

In the test, you'll be asked to add an attachment to an email. It's also useful to know how to save a document that has been attached to an email, although you won't be expected to do this in the test.

Attaching a file

1 To attach a file to an email in Microsoft® Outlook, click 'Attach File'.

2 Find the file you want to attach in your folder structure, click it, and then select 'Insert'.

You will then be able to see your document in the 'Attachments' area. In the test, you will need to take a screen shot as evidence.

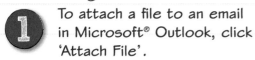
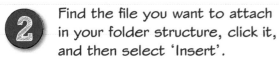

Saving an attached file

The paperclip symbol shows you that an email has an attachment.

1 To save an attachment, right-click the file name and click 'Save As'.

2 Navigate to the folder where you want to save the file, change the filename if you wish, and click 'Save'.

If there is more than one attachment, right-click one of the file names and select 'Save All Attachments...'.

Emailing large files

Some email providers only let you send and receive small files. If your attachment is too large, the email may not be delivered. You can reduce the size of an attachment by compressing it using a zipping tool. Alternatively, you could share the file using a cloud storage service.

Now try this

Compose an email to your own email address in Microsoft® Outlook or another email client.

- Write a suitable subject and message.
- Attach a file of your choice.
- When it arrives in your inbox, make sure you can successfully save the file to a new folder on your desktop.

Remember to include a message in your email explaining what the attachment is. Read the instructions in the test carefully as you may be asked to include specific details in the message.

Getting emails right

It is important to write a suitable message containing relevant information with a professional tone in every email. You will need to use correct spelling, grammar and punctuation in your email in the test.

Using the correct language

When you are sending an email to someone you do not know, you should:

- write clearly and in full sentences
- punctuate properly, with full stops and capital letters
- avoid using text language
- avoid using emoticons.

Your spelling is not being tested, but what you've written must make sense.

> You are allowed to bring a dictionary into the test, but try not to use it too much because it will take up valuable time.

Choosing a greeting

Use a greeting beginning with 'Dear...' followed by either a first name, or a title and surname.

✓ Dear John

✓ Dear Mr Smith

✗ Dear John Smith

If you don't know the person's name, use 'Dear Sir or Madam'.

It isn't appropriate to start a business email with 'Hi' or similar.

It is important to end your email with a sign-off. You can finish an email with 'Regards' followed by your name.

Getting it right

Read the question carefully to check what you need to include in your message.

✓ Make sure you choose an appropriate subject line that includes any important words from the question.

✓ If you've attached a file, make sure you say so. For example, 'I've attached my draft poster. Please let me have your comments.'

Golden rule

After you have written an email, you should read it carefully to check for mistakes or typos. Don't rely on the spell-checker because it may not pick up grammar and punctuation errors that make the message hard to understand.

Now try this

Rajiv Nayak is your manager at Dinglewood Motors, the garage you work for. He has asked you to produce a newsletter.

- Compose an email to Rajiv. His email address is rajiv@example.com
- Attach the file **NewsletterPG24L1**
- Paste a screen shot of your email into a new document, saved in a folder on your desktop with a suitable filename.

Safe and savvy online

The internet is an incredibly useful resource that keeps us all connected, but it is important to know how to keep yourself and others safe online.

Staying safe online

Follow these tips to stay safe online.

✓ Have **strong passwords** on social media accounts, and keep them secret.

✓ Your **online friends** should be people you know in real life. Remember that photos on social media websites may not be genuine.

✓ Don't put **personal details** on your public profile. This information could be used for identity theft.

✓ Report any online **bullying, threats and harassment**.

✓ Use the **privacy settings** on social media accounts to make sure only your friends can see your posts and profile.

✓ Set up **parental controls** to protect young people from seeing unsuitable websites.

✓ Use your email account's **junk filter** to avoid receiving emails you don't want to see.

Go to page 13 for more on passwords and viruses.

Suspicious emails

Never reply to emails that ask for personal details, such as your login to a website or your bank details.

If you receive an email with an unexpected link, don't click it. If you know the person who sent it, ask them what it is first. If you don't know the person who sent it, it's best to delete the email.

Netiquette

When you're online, it can be easy to type something that you wouldn't say to someone's face.

• Treat others with respect, even if you don't like their views.

• Do not post angry messages. This is known as trolling.

• Avoid typing in all capital letters – it's considered to be like shouting.

• Keep posts brief and check that they make sense.

• Think twice before posting something on the internet. Remember, once something is on the internet it can be around the world in seconds, copied via email and social media sites.

Now try this

You receive an email from Cranford Bank informing you that there is a problem with your bank account and asking you to confirm your identity by entering your username and password.
You have an account with Cranford Bank and use online banking. What should you do, and why?

Putting it into practice

For **Section B: Task 4**, you will be asked to prepare an email. After creating your email, always make sure that:

✓ the email address is spelled correctly

✓ the subject is appropriate

✓ you have attached the correct document

✓ the message makes sense and includes all the required information

✓ the language is appropriate, and spelling and grammar are correct.

You may **not** use the internet for this task.

Janey Smith runs a mobile spa business and has received the following email.

✉ send 📎 attach 💾 save

from: b.lehrer@example.co.uk

to: You

subject: Latest price list

Dear Ms Smith,

Please can you send me a copy of your latest price list for spa treatments and let me know whether you have an appointment available for a manicure next Wednesday afternoon?

Regards,
Ben Lehrer

 Remember to give your email a suitable subject.

 You should include a message in your email with all the important details given in the task information. Use a professional tone and correct spelling, grammar and punctuation.

- Prepare an email to the sender, attaching a copy of the document **PricesPG26L1**.

- Include a message telling Ben Lehrer you have a free appointment at 2 p.m. on Wednesday and ask if he would like to book it.

Evidence

- A document with a screen shot of the email that you have prepared.

Make sure your screen shot clearly shows the email address, the subject, the message and the attachment. It must be large enough for the text to be easily readable.

(6 marks)

Entering text

Microsoft® Word is a **word processing** application. It is used for documents that mostly involve text, such as posters, flyers, reports, essays, letters, memos and forms.

Opening Microsoft® Word

To open **Microsoft® Word**, type 'word' into the search box, and click on the app. Double-click the **Blank** template option to start a new document.

Getting it right

If you're familiar with Microsoft® Publisher (Desktop Publishing software), you can use it in your test to create a poster or flyer.

Your keyboard

Make sure that you know where these keys are on your keyboard.

Press the Caps Lock key to type all letters as uppercase.

Hold down the Shift key to type a capital letter.

Some keys have more than one function. To use the secondary function, hold down the key at the same time as the Control key.

Press the Tab key to move the cursor forward.

Press the Delete key to erase text to the right of the cursor.

Press the backspace key to erase text to the left of the cursor.

Press the Enter key to start a new paragraph.

Hold down the Shift key to use the symbols above the numbers.

Press the Space bar to move the cursor one space forward.

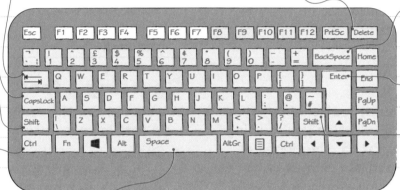

Adding and deleting text

To add text, click anywhere on the document to make the cursor (|) appear and start typing. To delete text, one character at a time, use the Delete or Backspace key. To delete entire words, sentences or paragraphs, click and drag to highlight the text you want to delete and press the Delete key.

Using Microsoft® Notepad

In your test, you might have to copy and paste text from a Microsoft® Notepad file.

Microsoft® Notepad is a simple text editing application. It doesn't allow you to apply formatting, so you will need to copy the text into Microsoft® Word and produce your document there. Maximise the Microsoft® Notepad window to ensure sure you select and copy all of the text.

Now try this

- Open the file **ShoppinglistPG27L1**
- Delete the date and change it to **4th August 2016**.
- Enter the text on the right beneath the date.
- Change **Cheese and tomato pizza** to **Cheese & tomato pizza**.
- Save the file with a meaningful name on the Desktop.

Cheese and tomato pizza   Bread
Milk (skimmed)   Eggs
Lettuce

Formatting text

Formatting text means changing the way it looks – its size, style and colour. It is used to emphasise important information or to make your page look more attractive and interesting.

You need to know how to:

- Change font style and size, such as from Times New Roman size 14 to Comic Sans size 8
- Use **bold**, underline, *italics* and highlighting
- Change font colour
- Change the case to CAPITAL LETTERS.

Golden rule

Avoid using WordArt: you need to demonstrate that you can use a range of text formatting techniques.

Selecting text

Remember to **select** text before you try to format it.

- To select a word, double-click it.
- To select a paragraph, double-click in the left margin next to it.
- To select all the text in your document, triple-click in the left margin.
- To select part of a sentence or paragraph, click and drag the cursor across the text, or click at the beginning then hold down the Shift key and click at the end.

How to do it

Formatting options may look slightly different depending on the application you're using. In Microsoft® Word 2013, the ribbon at the top of the screen has shortcuts to the formatting features you are likely to need most often.

font style   font size

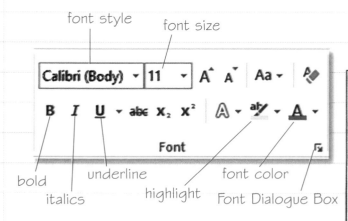

bold   italics   underline   highlight   font color   Font Dialogue Box

Choosing a font

You should use the same font for all of the main text in your document.

- Choose an easy-to-read **sans serif** font, such as Arial or Calibri. Avoid serif fonts, such as Times New Roman.
- You can choose a different font for the title and subheadings but make sure it is appropriate and don't use more than one.

Top tips for formatting

1 To combine formatting features easily, and use advanced options, click the tiny arrow in the bottom right corner of the font ribbon to open the font dialogue box.

2 To quickly copy formatting from one selection of text to another, use the Format Painter.

Now try this

Using Format Painter will help you work more quickly.

Make the following changes to the file **FormattingPG28L1**

- Format all the text as Comic Sans font.
- Make the heading: size 20, bold, dark green, and all upper case letters.
- Put the names of all the buildings in paragraph 1 into italics.
- Highlight in yellow the email address.

Page layout

As well as using formatting techniques to change the way text looks, you need to use layout features to improve the appearance of documents.

Layout basics

Templates

When you open Microsoft® Word, you'll see a selection of templates to choose from. For the test, use the 'Blank' template.

Page borders

To add a page border, choose the 'Design' tab and click 'Page Borders'. Select an 'Art' border from the drop-down menu and click 'OK'. There are also 'Box' borders, which are useful for business documents.

Margins

To change the size of the margins, choose 'Margins' on the 'Page Layout' tab. You can select one of the predefined options, or you can set 'Custom Margins'.

Orientation

To switch the layout of your paper from portrait to landscape, choose the 'Page Layout' tab at the top of the window and click 'Orientation'.

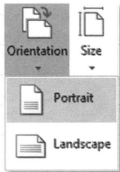

Lists

If you have a list of short, linked points, you can format them as bullet points.
If your list items are in a particular order, for example a set of instructions, you can format it as a numbered list.

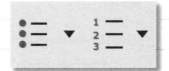

To create a new set of bullets, click the 'Bullets' icon and type the first line. Press the Enter key for each new bullet.

1 Highlight the lines you want to add bullet points to and click the 'Bullets' icon.

2 To add a new bullet point on the next line, press the Enter key.

3 To end the list, click the 'Bullets' icon again.

You can make a numbered list in the same way using the 'Numbering' icon, which is next to the 'Bullets' icon.

Alignment

You can use the alignment icons to position text to the left, in the centre or to the right of the page.

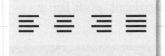

Headers and footers

In the test, you'll be asked to put your name, centre number and candidate number in the footer on all of your files.

1 Choose 'Footer' on the 'Insert' tab.

2 Select the three column layout and type in your details.

3 When you have finished typing, click 'Close Header and Footer'.

Now try this

- Open the file **PagelayoutPG29L1**
- Change the layout to **landscape**.
- Centre the heading 'Page layout'.
- Format the three points as a bulleted list.
- Add a footer to the document and type your name in it.

Using tables

A table is a grid made up of rows and columns, usually with headings at the top of each column and labels at the left of each row. You can use tables to present numbers, facts and figures in an organised way that makes them easy-to-read.

Creating a table

You need to know how to create a table.

On the 'Insert' tab, click the 'Table' icon.

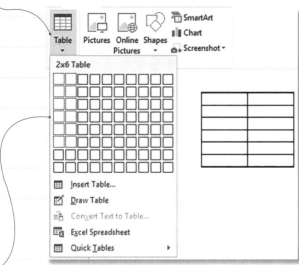

On the grid that appears, move your cursor right and down until the required number of columns and rows are highlighted orange. Click to select this size.

Your table will appear and you can type your data in the cells. Use the Tab key to move right across the rows.

Rows and columns

Resizing rows and columns

1 Move your pointer over the boundary between two columns or rows until it becomes a resizing symbol.

2 Click and drag to change the column width or row height.

Inserting rows and columns

1 Right-click a cell in the row or column next to where you would like to insert a new one.

2 From the drop-down menu, choose 'Insert' and then select the relevant option.

Deleting rows and columns

1 Use your mouse to select the cells in the row or column you want to delete.

2 Click the 'Delete' icon on the toolbar and choose 'Delete Columns' or 'Delete Rows'.

Formatting and layout

You can change the font and alignment of text in tables to make the table clear and easy-to-read.

To format text, use your mouse to highlight the contents of the cell, row, or column you want to change. A toolbar will appear.

You can also add a background colour to rows, columns and individual cells. To change the background colour, click the paint tin icon. Your table might be easier to read if you make alternate rows a different colour.

What can you use a table for?

Column headings (across) and row labels (down) are used to show clearly what the data is.

This table is part of a workout plan for a client at a gym.

Exercise	Sets	Time Each
Alternate heels	5	30 seconds
Bicycle crunches	3	60 seconds
Seated knee tucks	5	60 seconds
Side plank with knee pull	5	45 seconds
Weighted oblique static hold	3	30 seconds

3 columns

6 rows including the column headings

Now try this

Open the file **TablePG30L1** and use your formatting and layout skills to make it clear and easy-to-read.

Using images

In the test, you could be asked to place an image in a document. Read the question carefully to work out where you can find the image. You'll be given a folder containing some images, but you could be asked to use an image you found on the internet for Task 1.

Inserting an image

There are **two** ways to insert an image into a Microsoft® Word file.

1 If the image is saved on your computer, go to the 'Insert' tab and select 'Pictures'.

2 If the image is from the internet or another file, copy and paste it directly into your document.

Using Layout Options

You can use 'Layout Options' to position and arrange images in your document. The default setting is **In Line with Text**. To change the position of your image, select it, click the 'Layout Options' icon and choose:

- **Square** to wrap text around your image
- **Tight** to wrap text closely around an image
- **In front of text** to place image over text.

Make sure your images don't hide any text.

- -

Cropping

You can **crop** an image to remove unnecessary parts or blank space.

1 Right-click the image to bring up the formatting tool bar.

2 Click the crop icon.

3 Move the cursor over a cropping handle. The cursor will become T-shaped. Click, hold and push inwards to crop the image.

Resizing and rotating

To **resize** or **rotate** an image, click on the image to show its handles.

Use the circular handle above the image to rotate.

Use the **corner** handles to resize.

Golden rule

Only use the corner handles to resize an image. Otherwise, you might distort the image.

Now try this

- Open the file **ImagesPG31L1**
- Insert the image file **House** into this document.
- Resize and rotate the image.
- Crop the image so that the car isn't included in the final image.
- Save the file.

Using text boxes and shapes

You can improve the appearance of a document by using text boxes and shapes.

Text boxes

Text boxes are useful if you want to position some text in a particular bit of space in your document, or label a diagram.

Built-in

Simple Text Box

 Click where you want the text to be, go to the 'Insert' tab and choose 'Text Box'.

2 Choose the 'Simple Text Box' from the drop-down menu.

3 Replace the sample text with your own, and drag the text box to where you want it to be.

Resizing and rotating text boxes

Resizing and rotating text boxes is just like working with images, except that you don't need to worry about distorting the dimensions.

- Use the corner handles or the side handles to resize.
- Use the circular handle above the text box to rotate.
- Click the 'Layout Options' icon to change how the text box fits with the other text on the page.

Make sure all the text in a text box is visible. If the text box is too small for the amount of text, you will need to resize it.

Shapes

Shapes can make your document look more attractive. Shapes are especially appropriate for flyers and posters.

 Select 'Shapes' on the 'Insert' tab.

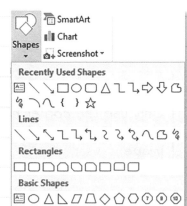

2 Choose the shape you want to use.

3 Click on the page then drag the cursor to draw the shape.

 Right-click on the shape to 'Add Text'.

Formatting text boxes and shapes

Select the 'Format' tab to display formatting options for text boxes and shapes.
For example, you can change the fill colour and the border.

You can use 'Layout Options' to change the way text boxes and shapes behave in the document, just as with images.

Go to page 31 for more about Layout Options.

Now try this

- Open a new Microsoft® Word document.
- Insert a circle and a text box.
- Resize the circle so it is 5 cm wide.
- Rotate the text box so it is at an angle.

Audience and purpose

When you create a document, make sure you consider the **audience** and **purpose**. You should choose formatting and layout features that are appropriate for both the type of document and the audience.

Formal or informal?

You must always consider the **audience** – who the document is for. Does the document need to be formal or informal? As well as using appropriate language, you should use appropriate formatting.

In a formal document:

- choose plain sans serif fonts
- use mainly black and white, with a few colours if suitable
- use tables to display information clearly.

In an informal document:

- use colours (but not too many) to make the document more appealing
- choose interesting fonts (but make sure they are still easy-to-read).

Types of document

Here are some examples of documents you could be asked to create in the test:

- newsletter
- fact sheet
- poster
- advert
- leaflet
- invitation
- flyer
- letter
- report
- meeting minutes.

Designing for purpose

You also need to think about the **purpose** of the document.

If a document is intended to provide information, such as a report or a letter:

- present the information in a simple, professional way
- make sure you have included all the information the reader needs.

If a document is intended to attract attention, such as a poster or a flyer:

- use large, bold fonts to attract attention
- use colour and images to make it eye-catching
- keep the text clear and concise.

Appropriate designs

Make sure that any formatting features that you use are there for a reason and enhance the document.

Think about how your document would look printed out.

- Have you used dark text on a light background?
- Does the design fill the page, no large areas of white space?
- Is the font easy-to-read?
- Is the title larger than the main body text?

Go to pages 34-36 to revise creating a range of documents.

Now try this

1 Name **three** types of formatting you could use in a formal document.
2 What **two** things should you bear in mind when using colour and interesting fonts in an informal document?

Posters and adverts

You could be asked to create a poster or an advert. The main purpose of these documents is to attract attention and provide key information.

Features of a poster or advert

formatting techniques, such as colour and shapes, used to attract attention (not WordArt)

headings larger than body text to make them stand out

large font sizes so text can be read from a distance

Dinglewood Soup Kitchen

Volunteers needed

Do you want to make a difference in your community?

Dinglewood Soup Kitchen needs your help.

Starting from **Saturday June 4th**

Every Saturday

11 a.m. to 3 p.m.

Dinglewood Community Centre

- -

For more information contact us:
dinglewoodsc@example.com

suitable image, sensibly positioned and sized

text is clear and concise

text enhancements, such as underline and bold, used to highlight key information

no large areas of empty space

Document size

You could be asked to produce a document that is a particular size, for example no larger than A5. To change the page size, use the 'Size' button on the 'Page Layout' tab. If the option you need isn't listed, choose 'More Paper Sizes...' then select 'Custom Size' and input the page dimensions you need.

Getting it right

Read the question carefully and follow all of the instructions. If the question gives you a layout plan to follow, make sure you use it!

Now try this

Create a poster about health and safety in the workplace. The poster should:

- include text from the file **PosterPG34L1** and add a text box with one important tip.
- include a suitable image
- be clear, easy-to-read and suitable for its audience and purpose.

 Remember to check for spelling errors and remove any text that isn't needed.

Newsletters, leaflets and flyers

You could be asked to create a newsletter, factsheet, flyer or leaflet. The main purpose of these documents is to provide information in an attractive way.

Features of a newsletter, leaflet or flyer

text formatting, such as bold and colour, used to add visual appeal

no large areas of empty space

headings and subheadings used to break text into sections

images positioned neatly and positioned next to the relevant text

headings larger than body text

formatting techniques, such as bulleted lists and columns, used to present information clearly

more information than a poster

Beecham College News

Welcome to the summer issue of Beecham College News.

We are now just weeks away from the summer holidays and I hope you all enjoy a well-deserved break.

Read on to find out more about what everyone's been up to this term.

Work Placements

This term many of you tested your skills on work experience. Students were placed in all kinds of exciting industries, from construction to fitness and childcare.

Jessica Peak spent two weeks with a local engineering firm. "It was great to get involved in real life projects and try out the things I've learned at college" she said.

The employers all said that the students were a credit to Beecham.

Fundraising

June was National Fundraising Month, and we challenged you to raise money for three new computers for the library.

The response was brilliant. Catering students sold delicious cakes, the Health and Fitness classes had a charity football tournament, and many of you joined in a sponsored walk around Beecham forest.

All together you raised an amazing £2,159 – well done!

Sports

- The boy's football team finished second in the league.
- The girl's football team have been promoted to Division 1.
- Badminton ace Naresh Chaudhary is taking part in the National Championships next month – good luck!

Using columns

You can use columns to make large sections of text easier to read. Columns are most appropriate for newsletters and leaflets.

 Select the text you want to format.

 On the 'Page Layout' tab, click 'Columns'.

 Choose the number of columns you want from the drop-down menu.

Leaflet layouts

You might need to think about how a leaflet would be folded. For example, to create a folded A4 leaflet, you could create a landscape A4 document and format the text into two or four columns.

 To undo column formatting, select the text then set the number of columns to one.

Now try this

Using the text from the file **KitchensPG35L1**, create an A4 factsheet about fitted kitchens to give to customers at the DIY store you work for.

- Use formatting to produce a document that is attractive, easy-to-read and draws attention to key information. Include the image **Kitchens**.
- Save the file with a suitable name.

Letters and business documents

You could be asked to create a letter or other business document. The main purpose of a letter or business document is to communicate information in a clear and professional way.

Features of a letter

Letters need to be formatted in a specific way. When you create a letter, make sure you include all of these features.

recipient's address on the left

formal greeting, starting with 'Dear' and one of:
- recipient's first name
- recipient's title and surname
- Sir/Madam

text organised into paragraphs and left aligned

Looks Beautiful
Hair and beauty supplies

2, Something Street
Anytown
Countyshire
CS2 0ZZ

Beauty Etc Wholesale Supplies
Dinglewood
Countyshire
CS2 5UH

April 15th 2016

Subject: Agent visit

Dear Mr Barker

Please could you arrange for one of your representatives to visit us in the near future with a range of sample hair products? We are considering stocking some new lines, and a number of your products are of interest.

We are in a prime position and have a high turnover, so would be looking for your very best prices.

Any Wednesday afternoon would suit us: no appointment necessary.

Yours sincerely,

J Smithers
Manager

Looks Beautiful
Hair and beauty supplies

sender's address in the top right corner

today's date

subject line to say what the letter is about

sign-off, such as:
- 'Yours sincerely' if you have used the recipient's name
- 'Yours faithfully' if you have not

space for a signature

name and role of the sender

Business documents

Follow the same principles for other business documents, such as meeting minutes or reports. For these document types, make sure you format headings to stand out.

Golden rule

Keep formatting simple! You could add a plain border or use a bulleted list, but stick to plain fonts and avoid fancy borders, shapes and unnecessary colour. Leave the text black so that it is easy-to-read.

Now try this

Your manager asks you to produce a letter addressed to all employees.
- Create the letter using the text in **PartyPG36L1**
- Include an appropriate image from the folder **Drinks**
- Save the file with a suitable name.

Checking your work

You should always check any documents you produce to make sure they are accurate and suitable for the audience and purpose. In the test, it is also important to check that you've done what is asked.

Key things to check

1 Have you considered your audience and purpose?

2 Are the page borders and font style appropriate?

3 Is your work all on one page (if it should be)?

4 Is the orientation (portrait or landscape) what was asked for?

5 Have you added a header or footer (if they were asked for)?

6 Is the layout balanced, or is there too much empty white space?

7 Have you included the relevant images, in the appropriate places?

Spelling and grammar

This isn't an English test, but your work must make sense. Let Microsoft® Word check the spelling and grammar, but make sure you also read any text carefully yourself, too.

You may need to make something smaller or delete additional space if necessary.

You may need to enlarge images or increase the size of headings and body text to fill empty space.

Appropriate formatting

In the test you could be asked to make sure your document is **clear, easy-to-read** and **informative** (or words to that effect).

Check that:

- text is a sensible size and in an easy-to-read font
- headings and subheadings are bigger than body text
- key information is formatted to stand out
- text is not hidden by images or narrow table columns.

Copying text accurately

If you are copying text from a Microsoft® Notepad file, make sure you delete any notes that are there for your benefit. For example:

✗ This event is held every August [insert the month name you found in Task 1] in Bristol.

✗ This event is held every [August] in Bristol.

✓ This event is held every August in Bristol.

Now try this

- Open the document **PaintPG37L1**
- Use formatting to make the document informative, clear and easy-to-read.
- Save the file with a suitable name.

Putting it into practice

For **Task 3**, you will be asked to produce a document that brings together some text from a Microsoft® Notepad file, the information you found in Section A, and one or more images. Make sure you do the following.

✓ Read the question carefully.

✓ Follow all instructions.

✓ Take care when saving files. Give them sensible names and save them where you can find them!

✓ Check your answers.

1 You may **not** use the internet for this task.

Brandleton Nursery wants to produce some fact sheets for parents about child development.

Produce a fact sheet to give parents information on what to expect in the first three months after having a baby.

The fact sheet must be:

- one A4 page
- clear and easy to read
- suitable for parents.

It must include:

- the text from **MilestonesPG38L1**
- two other appropriate images and a logo selected from **ImagesPG38L1**
- the information you found in **Task 1**
- the cost of producing each fact sheet that you calculated in **Section B, Task 2**.

> Notice that the audience for the fact sheet is parents rather than children. Make sure keep the audience in mind.

> Underline the important parts of the instructions to help you remember to include everything you are asked to.

> As Task 1 is not part of this practice exercise, the information you need is: 48 hours.

> As Task 2 is not part of this practice exercise, the information you need is: 15p

Evidence

A copy of your fact sheet saved in a new folder on your desktop.

> Enter your name, candidate number and centre number in the footer. Save the fact sheet with a meaningful file name.

(4 marks)

See page 35 for useful tips.

What are spreadsheets?

Spreadsheet applications allow you to organise, sort and present data, and perform calculations quickly and accurately. This guide uses Microsoft® Excel 2013.

What does a spreadsheet look like?

This is the sort of spreadsheet you could be working with in your test. It shows a shop's weekly takings for the different categories of goods it sells.

Each box in the grid is called a 'cell'. Every cell has an 'address', which is made up of the letter of its column, and the row number, e.g. D5. If you click on a cell, the address appears in the 'name' box.

Tables should always have a suitable heading.

The row labels (in Column A) are usually formatted differently to the column headings.

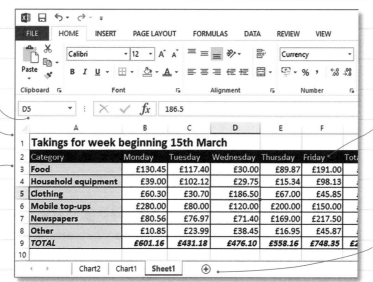

Column headings are formatted to make them stand out.

You can add a worksheet to your workbook by clicking the + icon. You won't be expected to use this feature in the test.

Category	Monday	Tuesday	Wednesday	Thursday	Friday	Tot...
Food	£130.45	£117.40	£30.00	£89.87	£191.00	
Household equipment	£39.00	£102.12	£29.75	£15.34	£98.13	
Clothing	£60.30	£30.70	£186.50	£67.00	£45.85	
Mobile top-ups	£280.00	£80.00	£120.00	£200.00	£150.00	
Newspapers	£80.56	£76.97	£71.40	£169.00	£217.50	
Other	£10.85	£23.99	£38.45	£16.95	£45.87	
TOTAL	£601.16	£431.18	£476.10	£558.16	£748.35	£2

Workbooks and worksheets

Files that you create in spreadsheet applications are called 'workbooks'. Workbooks contain 'worksheets', which you can see in the bottom left corner of the screen. You can move to a different worksheet by clicking on the tab.

Go to pages 50-55 to revise producing graphs and charts.

What can you use spreadsheets for?

Spreadsheets are useful for many different purposes. They are best for managing a lot of numbers, for example:

- keeping track of your personal budget
- creating an invoice
- tracking scores at a sports event
- storing the results of a survey.

Go to pages 50-55 to revise producing graphs and charts.

Now try this

- Open the file **TakingsPG39L1**
- What figure is in cell G7?
- What is the cell address for **Clothing?**
- Close the file without saving the changes.

Entering and changing data

You need to be able to enter data into a spreadsheet and edit data that's already there.

Entering data

You can **enter** data by clicking on a cell to select it and typing. To move to a different cell, you can use the mouse to click on a new cell, or use the arrow keys on your keyboard to move there.

Getting it right

Make sure you enter data carefully. When you have finished inputting data into a spreadsheet, double check that all the data matches the data you were given.

Changing data

If you need to **change** the data in a cell, you can do any of the following.

- Click on the cell to select it and start typing to replace all of the text in the cell.
- Double-click the cell to get a flashing cursor and edit the number or word(s).
- Click in the formula bar, which shows the contents of the active cell, and type to change the text.

Copying and pasting cells

To copy a cell, select the cell and do one of the following.

- Hold Ctrl and C on the keyboard.
- Click the 'Copy' icon on the ribbon.
- Right-click on the cell then select 'Copy' from the drop-down menu.

The cell will be surrounded by a moving border. You can press Esc to cancel.

To paste the contents in another cell, select that cell and do one of the following.

- Hold Ctrl and V on the keyboard.
- Click the 'Paste' icon on the ribbon.
- Right-click then select 'Paste' from the drop-down menu.

Cutting and pasting cells

You can cut and paste a cell instead of copying it. This moves the contents of the cell, leaving the original cell empty. To cut a cell, select the cell then do one of the following.

- Hold Ctrl and X on the keyboard.
- Click the 'Cut' icon on the ribbon.
- Right-click on the cell then select 'Cut' from the drop-down menu.

Go to page 27 to revise keyboard functions.

Now try this

- Open the file **TakingsPG40L1**
- Change the following information in the spreadsheet.
  - The row label 'Clothes' should say 'Clothing'.
  - The figures for 'Mobile top-ups' have been missed off. They are: 80, 120, 200, 150.
  - The figure for 'Newspapers' on 'Friday' should have been 217.50.
- Save the file with a suitable name.

Rows and columns

For the spreadsheet task, you could be asked to add and delete rows and columns.
You may also need to resize rows and columns to make sure that no text or data is cut off.

Adding columns and rows

1 Select the column or row immediately after where you want to add a new column or row.

2 Right-click on the grey bar and choose 'Insert'.

Deleting columns and rows

1 Select the column or row you want to delete.

2 Right-click on the grey bar and choose 'Delete'.

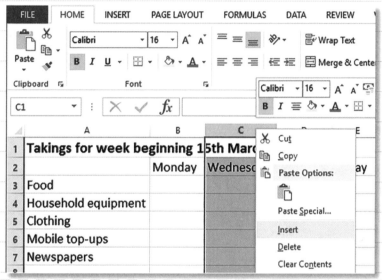

Adjusting height and width

You may need to adjust the size of your rows and columns to fit your data.

1 Select the column or row.

2 Drag the border to increase or decrease the height or width.

> All rows except the headings row should be the same depth.

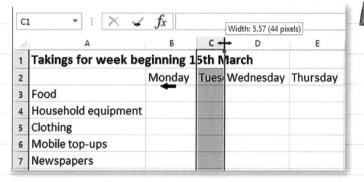

Now try this

> You will need to adjust column widths to ensure that all of the data is visible.

- Open the spreadsheet **TakingsPG41L1**
- Delete the 'Toys' row.
- Add another row above the 'Total' row, with the label 'Other'.
- Add in the figures for Monday to Friday: 10.85, 23.99, 38.45, 16.95, 45.87.
- Make sure all of the data is visible.

Formatting data

You need to format text, numbers and the layout to make information clear and easy to understand.

Formatting key information

You should use formatting to make key information stand out.

- Increase the size of the title, e.g. 14 pt.
- Make column headings and row labels bold.
- Make averages and totals bold and italic.
- Change the fill and font colour of headings, labels, totals and averages.
- Add a border around key data, or around all the data.

Formatting cells, rows and columns

1 To apply formatting to a cell, select the cell and use the formatting options on the 'Home' tab.

2 To apply formatting to more than one cell, click and drag to highlight the cells and select the formatting option.

3 To apply formatting to an entire row or column, click the grey bar and select the formatting option.

Formatting numbers

You can display numbers as percentages, dates and currency by applying number formats in Microsoft® Excel.

If there are dates in a spreadsheet, you can present them as a short date (15/01/2016) or a long date (15 January 2016).

ABC 123	General — No specific format
12	Number
	Currency
	Accounting
	Short Date
	Long Date
	Time
%	Percentage
½	Fraction
10²	Scientific
	More Number Formats...

1 Select the cells you want to format.

2 Click the arrow next to 'General' on the 'Home' tab.

3 Select the format you want to use, for example 'Currency'.

You can also change the number of decimal places showing and separate thousands with a comma by selecting 'More Number Formats'.

Getting it right

In the test, you should format the data after you've completed the other steps. Check that formatting is consistent. Avoid unnecessary formatting, such as using too much colour.

If you see ##### in a cell after you apply number formatting to it, the cell isn't wide enough. Widen the column to see the data.

Go to page 41 to revise resizing rows and columns.

Now try this

- Open the spreadsheet **TakingsPG42L1**
- Make sure the data is clear and easy to read:
  - Make the column headings and row labels bold.
  - Make the column heading white on a black background.
  - Display all money as currency with 2 decimal places.
  - In cell K3, add the date the shop started trading, 15/01/16. Display it as a long date.
- Save the file with a suitable name.

Using simple formulas

In the test, you need to show that you can use simple formulas to add, subtract, multiply and divide.

Using simple formulas

1 To start any formula, type an equals sign (=) in the cell you want the answer to appear in.

2 Type the address of the cell where the first number is, or just click on the cell to put its address in the formula.

3 Type the maths operator (+, -, *, /).

4 Type the address of the cell where the second number is, or click on its cell.

5 Press Enter to display the answer.

If you change the number in any of the cells used in the formula, the answer will change, too.

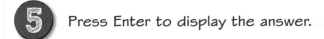

| A1 | fx | Simple formulas |

	A	B	C	D
1	Simple formulas			
2	Calculation	Formula		
3	Addition	= C3 + D3	20	30
4	Subtraction	= C4 - D4	30	20
5	Multiplication	= C5 * D5	8	9
6	Division	= C6/D6	50	5

Choosing the right symbol

Choose the symbol for multiplying and dividing carefully:

| / | ✓ | ÷ | ✗ |
| * | ✓ | × | ✗ |

Replicating a formula

Rather than writing out the same formula over and over again, you can **replicate** it.

Microsoft® Excel will work out what the cell addresses in each answer cell should be (although you should check them yourself).

To replicate a formula:

- click the cell that contains the formula you want to copy
- click and hold the black square in the bottom right corner of the cell
- drag the cursor to copy the formula into other cells.

Getting it right

In the test, you may need to include more than one type of calculation within your formula. Think carefully about the order that you write the calculations in as it could affect the answer.

| DAY | fx | =B3+C3 |

	A	B	C	D
1	Weekend takings in April			
2		Saturday	Sunday	Total
3	Week 1	£130.45	£191.99	=B3+C3
4	Week 2	£102.12	£290.75	
5	Week 3	£117.40	£211.59	
6	Week 4	£198.40	£211.59	

Now try this

 Remember to start every formula with an equals sign.

Your manager has started a spreadsheet to show the total cost of three orders for plumbing materials he has placed this month.

- Open the file **TanksPG43L1**
- For each order, multiply the **Number purchased** by the **Price each** to get the **Total cost**.
- Subtract the **Discount** he is getting on each order to find the **Net cost**.
- Save the file with a suitable name.

SUM, MIN and MAX

You can perform calculations in spreadsheet applications quickly, easily and accurately using functions such as SUM, MIN and MAX. Functions are ready-made formulas designed to save you time.

Ranges

You need to know how to do a calculation that involves lots of cells, for example finding the total of the cell contents in a column. You can use a **range** instead of typing the address of every cell. For example, B3:B7 means all of the cells from B3 to B7. You can select a range by clicking the first cell and dragging across or down.

D9	▼	:	✕	✓	f_x	=SUM(D3:D8)

	A	B	C	D
1	**Takings for week beginning 15th March**			
2	Category	Monday	Tuesday	Wednesday
3	Food	£130.45	£117.40	£30.00
4	Household equipment	£39.00	£102.12	£29.75
5	Clothing	£60.30	£30.70	£186.50
6	Mobile top-ups	£280.00	£80.00	£120.00
7	Newspapers	£80.56	£76.97	£71.40
8	Other	£10.85	£23.99	£38.45
9	**TOTAL**	**£601.16**	**£431.18**	**£476.10**

Finding the total

To find a total efficiently, you can use the SUM function.

 Click in the cell where you want the answer to appear and type =SUM

 Type an opening bracket.

 Select the range of cells you want it to add. Hold down the Control key to select cells that aren't next to each other, to include them in the range.

 Type the closing bracket.

 Press Enter to display the answer.

When to use the SUM function

Use the SUM function:

✓ to add a **range** of cells.

Don't use the SUM function:

✗ to add 2 numbers together
✗ to subtract
✗ to multiply
✗ to divide.

Finding the highest and lowest values

To find the highest or lowest (maximum or minimum) in a set of numbers (a row, column, or any range), Microsoft® Excel has the functions =MAX and =MIN. They are used in exactly the same way as =SUM.

If you are calculating the MAX and MIN values, take care not to include the total!

Shortcuts

Microsoft® Excel has some useful shortcuts to help speed things up.

 Select the cell where you want the answer.

 Click the 'Autosum' button on the 'Home' tab to automatically perform the SUM function. Alternatively, choose one of the other options from the drop-down menu, including MIN, MAX and AVERAGE.

Now try this

- Open the file **SalonPG44L1**
- Use SUM to calculate a total for Column C on Row 8. Replicate this formula for the other services.
- Use SUM to calculate a total cost for Mrs Fairfax. Replicate this formula for the other clients.
- Use =MAX and =MIN to find the clients who spend the most and the least amount of money.
- Save the file with a suitable name.

Averages

Just as Microsoft® Excel has a function to calculate totals, it also has a function to calculate the average, =AVERAGE. However, if a question uses the word average, it doesn't always mean you can use =AVERAGE function.

What's an average?

You may remember from maths lessons that you can find out the **average** of a set of numbers (the mean) by adding them together and dividing by how many numbers there are.

Finding the average

1 Click in the cell where you want the average to be calculated.

2 Type =AVERAGE

3 Type an opening bracket.

4 Select the cells you want to find the average of.

5 Type a closing bracket.

6 Press Enter to display the average.

Here, you want to know the average weekly takings for food.

E3	▼	:	✕ ✓ fx	=AVERAGE(B3:D3)	
	A	B	C	D	E
1	**Weekend takings**				
2	Category	Friday	Saturday	Sunday	Average
3	Food	£130.45	£191.99	£89.97	£137.47
4	Household equipment	£102.12	£290.75	£97.89	
5	Clothing	£117.40	£211.59	£108.45	
6					

You could replicate the calculation for Household equipment and clothing by clicking the bottom right corner of the cell and dragging down to highlight H4 and H5.

When not to use =AVERAGE

One of the most common mistakes is using the =AVERAGE function when you have already calculated, or been given, the total for the range of cells. In these circumstances, part of the calculation of the average has already been done. All that's left for you to do is to divide the total by the number of values in the range. Look at the spreadsheet below to see an example.

The total weight of the bags has already been found. You just need to divide that by the number of bags to find the average weight.

Using =AVERAGE wouldn't give you the correct answer.

DAY	▼	:	✕ ✓ fx	= B2/C2	
	A	B	C	D
1	Supplier	Number of bags	Total weight (kg)	Average weight (kg)
2	Smiths	15	390.69	= B2/C2
3	AJT	40	999.99	
4	GRDS Ltd	60	1450.64	
5	Lots of Sand	30	889.75	

Now try this

- Open the spreadsheet **TakingsPG45L1** and resave it with a new name.
- Use suitable functions to complete:
  - the 'total' row
  - the 'total' column
  - the 'average' column.

Sorting and filtering

You may need to **sort** the rows or columns in a spreadsheet into a different order, for example, alphabetical order, date order or numerical order. You may also need to **filter** your data so that, instead of seeing all the data, you only see the data that you are interested in.

Spreadsheet language

First, make sure you understand these key words.

- A row in a spreadsheet table is called a **record**.

- A column in a spreadsheet table is called a **field**.

Getting it right

In the test, it's a good idea to save a copy of your formatted file before you start sorting or filtering, so you have the original to go back to if something goes wrong.

Filtering records

Filtering records doesn't delete or rearrange them – it hides the ones you don't want to see:

 Click on any column heading in your table.

 Click the 'sort and filter' icon.

 Choose 'filter'.

A drop-down menu appears on **every** column heading.

Use the drop-down menu to apply a filter.

To filter the records so only female employees are showing, click on the arrow next to 'Gender' in B1, untick 'Select all' and tick 'F'.

To restore hidden rows, click the drop-down menu on the column you have filtered and choose 'Clear filter'.

	A	B	C	D	E
1	Volunteer ID	Gender	Name	Role	Home
2	1001	F	Helen Leigh	Security	Manchester
3	1002	F	Jacinda Penter	Bar assistant	Liverpool
5	1004	F	Eva Grey	Ticket collector	Sunderland
9	1008	F	Emily Cale	Cleaner	Bournemouth
10					

Sorting records

Sorting records rearranges them into a particular numerical or alphabetical order:

 Click on any column heading in your table.

 Click the 'Sort and Filter' icon.

 Choose 'Sort A to Z' or 'Sort Z to A'.

To sort by numbers so that the smallest is at the top, click 'Sort A to Z'.
To sort numbers so that the highest is at the top, click 'Sort Z to A'. This also works for sorting dates.

To rearrange the records so that the employees' home towns are in alphabetical order, select the column heading 'Home' in F1 and choosing 'sort A to Z' from the 'Sort & Filter' options.

The whole records (entire rows) are rearranged, not just the text in the 'Home' column.

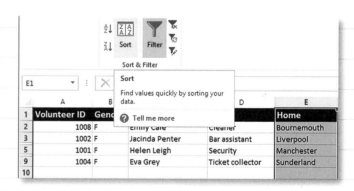

Now try this

- Open the spreadsheet **StaffListPG46L1**
- Sort the employee records in alphabetical order by **Job role**.
- Filter the sorted list to show only the males.
- Save the file with a sensible name.

Viewing and printing formulas

If an answer in your spreadsheet looks wrong, you may want to take a look at all the formulas so you can check them. You'll also need to print your formulas if you're doing the paper version of the test.

Displaying formulas

You can see a formula for one cell by clicking the cell and looking in the formula bar.
To display all the formulas in a spreadsheet you can either:

- click 'Show formulas' on the 'Formulas' tab

- hold down the Control key while you press the Grave accent key, which is normally above the Tab key.

Both of these options take you to 'Formula view'. To return to normal view, repeat either of these two steps.

Inserting a footer

You will need to insert a footer to your spreadsheet with your name, candidate number and centre number.

1 Click the 'View' tab and choose 'Page Layout'.

2 Scroll to the bottom of the page and click in the text box that is labelled 'Click to add footer'.

3 Type your details.

4 Return to your data by selecting 'Normal' on the 'View' tab.

Printing spreadsheets

If you are asked to print evidence of your work, you should check that the entire spreadsheet fits on the page. Look for a vertical and horizontal dashed line on your spreadsheet to see what will fit on one page when printed.

You may need to change the 'Print settings' to make your spreadsheet fit the page.

1 Select 'File'.

2 Click 'Print'.

3 Change the page orientation to landscape.

If the spreadsheet is still too wide to fit on one page you can change the scaling.

1 Select 'File'.

2 Click 'Print'.

3 Change the scaling to 'Fit Sheet on One Page'. This will print your spreadsheet in a smaller font to make it fit on one page, but will not affect the original.

Now try this

- Open the spreadsheet **ReceptionPG47L1**
- Use one of the methods above to show the data in formula view.
- Identify and change the incorrect formula in the spreadsheet.
- Print the spreadsheet in formula view on one sheet, making sure that all formulas are visible.
- Return to normal view.

Putting it into practice

In the test, you'll be provided with a simple spreadsheet, which you'll need to make some changes to. You could be asked to:

- add or delete rows and columns
- add, delete or change data
- use formulas
- format the data so that it's clear and easy-to-read.

 You may **not** use the internet from this point onwards.

The file **BrickSuppliesPG48L1** contains information on some brick purchases that your firm is making for a new construction project.

(a) Open the file **BrickPG48SuppliesL1**

- Enter your name, candidate number and centre number in the footer.
- Format all money amounts as currency to two decimal places.

(b) Some of the information is incorrect. Change the following information in the spreadsheet.

- The pack size for Antique finish bricks should be 120.
- The cost of a pack of Recycled bricks should be £196.

(1 mark)

 Always complete the tasks in order.

(c) Use a formula to calculate the cost per brick for each type of brick. The **Cost per brick** is **Cost of pack** divided by **Pack size**. Complete this column and use a formula to show the overall **Total cost** in cell **F12**.

(1 mark)

 Use the SUM function to calculate totals efficiently.

(d) Use a formula to include the average cost per brick in cell **D12**.

(1 mark)

(e) Sort the spreadsheet in **descending** order of total cost.

(1 mark)

(f) Make sure that the spreadsheet is easy to understand and that it fits on one page.

(1 mark)

 If you're doing the paper test, you may be asked to print your spreadsheet at different stages. Switch to formula view if you're asked to print formulas.

Evidence

- A copy of your completed spreadsheet.
- A printout of the formula view.

Types of charts and graphs

Charts and graphs are used to show tables of numbers in a visual way, making it easy to compare figures. You need to know how to produce bar charts, pie charts and line graphs, and when it is appropriate to use them.

Pie charts

Pie charts are circles that are split into different-sized sectors, representing data as a percentage of a whole. If the question uses words like **share**, **proportions**, or **breakdown**, you should use a pie chart.

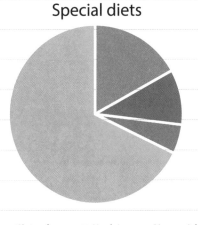

Special diets

■ Vegetarian   ■ Gluten free   ■ No dairy   ■ No special requirements

Column and bar charts

If you need to compare lots of categories, a column or bar chart might work better than a pie chart. These charts help you see every category clearly and notice any patterns.

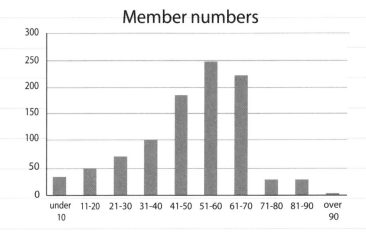

Member numbers

Line graphs

Line graphs are used to show how one thing relates to another, such as changes over time. A line connects each plotted point to the next one to show the pattern.

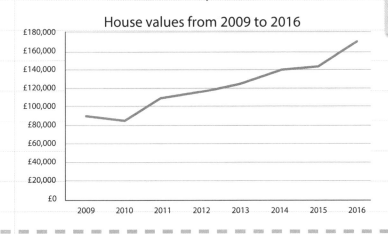

House values from 2009 to 2016

Getting it right

Think carefully about what sort of chart to produce in the test. When you've created it, take a good look to make sure your choice makes sense.

Go to pages 51–53 to revise creating the different types of charts and graphs.

Now try this

Name the chart or graph that would most effectively represent:

(a) the temperature variations in a hallway during the day

(b) the number of holidays each person in an office has taken in a year

(c) the proportion of time spent answering emails compared to other work tasks.

Selecting data for a chart

When you are creating a chart or graph, it is important to select the right cells. Here are some useful tips on how to get it right.

Selecting data

To create a chart you need to select a **range** of data.

- You can include all the data in your table, by clicking on one corner of your table and dragging the mouse until all of the data is selected.

- You can select non-adjacent rows, columns or ranges within your table by holding down the 'Control' key. Don't hold it down until after you've selected the first range of data.

Getting it right

Read the task carefully, so you know exactly what data you should be including in your chart or graph. If something goes wrong with your chart, delete it and try again.

Choosing a chart or graph

Once you have selected your data, choose the 'Insert' tab and click the type of graph you would like to use.

What you should include

Make sure you include the column headings and row labels. These will automatically be used as labels for your chart.

If you have a 'total' cell, make sure you don't include it. This is particularly important in a pie chart, where it will be listed as one of the categories and will change all of your proportions.

Go to page 51–53 to revise different charts and graphs.

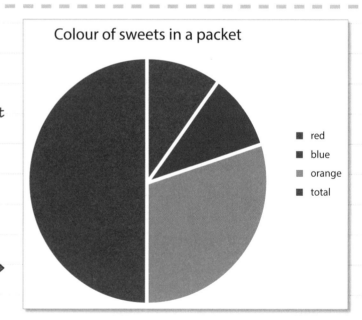

Colour of sweets in a packet

- red
- blue
- orange
- total

Now try this

- Open the spreadsheet **SalesPG50L1**
- Produce a simple chart showing the January and April figures for all six salespeople.
- Save the file with a suitable name.

Pie charts

In the test, you should insert a pie chart if you want to show proportions of a whole. For a pie chart, there can only be one set of data, and its labels.

Creating a pie chart

1 Select the data you want to represent. Make sure you select all of the columns or rows you need, including headings and labels.

2 On the 'Insert' tab, click the button that shows a pie chart and select the first option in the '2-D Pie' section.

3 To give the chart a title, double-click the text box to type in it. Make sure the title explains what the graph shows. The wording of the task might help you to choose a title.

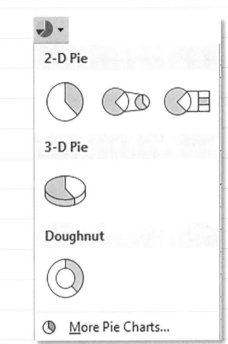

Pie chart tips

You can only make a pie chart from one column or row of data. Don't include the total or average of the data if it's there. You must include the column heading or row label.

A pie chart

Look at the pie chart and the data below. All the important information in the table has been included in the pie chart to make it easy to understand.

Subject	Number of students
ICT	50
Maths	88
English	70

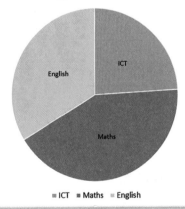

Students taking Functional Skills subjects

■ ICT ■ Maths ■ English

> Go to page 54 for more on moving and formatting charts.

Now try this

- Open the spreadsheet **TakingsPG51L1** and resave it with a new name.
- Create a pie chart showing a breakdown of the total between the categories.
- Give your chart a suitable title.

You'll need to select A3:A8 and K3:K8.

Column and bar charts

Column and bar charts display data visually as vertical or horizontal columns, making it easy to compare the relative size of data in different categories.

Creating a column or bar chart

1 Select the data you want to represent. Make sure you select all of the columns or rows you need, including headings and labels.

2 On the 'Insert' tab, click the button that shows a column chart or a bar chart. Choose the first option in the '2-D Column' or '2-D Bar' section depending on which chart you want to produce.

3 Make sure your chart has an appropriate title and axes labels.

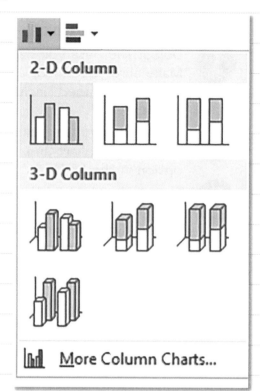

Golden rule

Always remember to select the data you want to represent carefully. Don't include any totals unless the question specifically asks you to.

A column chart

Look at the column chart and the data below. All the important information in the table has been included in the column chart to make it easy to understand.

Office supplies	Yearly spend
printer ink	£400.00
paper	£280.00
pens	£15.00
staples	£8.00
tea/coffee	£50.00
IT equipment	£500.00

Go to page 54 for more on formatting and moving charts.

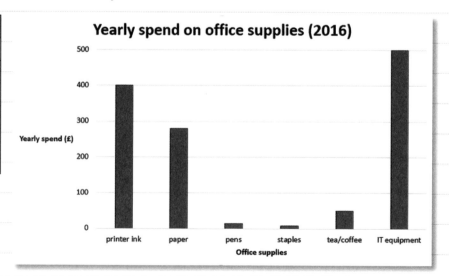

Now try this

- Open the spreadsheet **TakingsPG52L1** and resave it with a new name.
- Create a column chart showing the daily figures for 'Food' only.
- Give your chart a suitable title.

Line graphs

If you are asked to create a graph or chart to represent data about how something changes over time, you should use a line graph.

Creating a line graph

1 To create a line graph, select all of the data you want to represent. Make sure you select all of the columns or rows you need, including headings and labels.

2 On the 'Insert' tab, choose the line graph button and select the first option in the '2-D Line' section.

3 Change the title by double-clicking it to bring up the cursor.

Depending on your data, you might have more than one line on your graph.

A line graph

Look at the line graph and the data below. All the important information in the table has been included in the line graph to make it easy to understand.

Month	Temperature (°C)
January	4
February	6
March	6
April	12
May	16
June	20
July	26
August	22
September	20
October	13
November	8
December	2

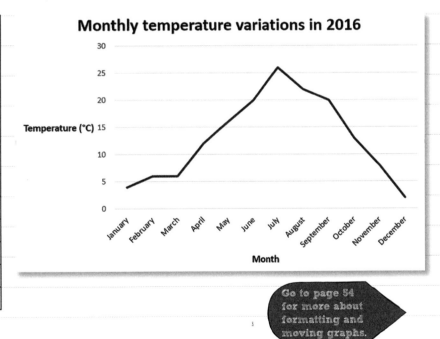

Monthly temperature variations in 2016

Go to page 54 for more about formatting and moving graphs.

Now try this

- Open the spreadsheet **PopulationPG53L1** and resave it with a new name.
- Produce a line graph showing how the population of **Castle Mowland** has changed since 1900.
- Give your chart a suitable title.

Formatting charts and graphs

When you have created your graph or chart, you need to format it to make sure it is clear and easy to understand. A well presented chart of graph that is easy to understand must include an appropriate title and axes labels.

Formatting options

You may need to make changes to your graph or chart to make it easier to understand.
To make changes, you can click on:

- the edge of the box to bring up the 'Design' and 'Format' tabs in the ribbon under the title 'Chart Tools'
- the title, labels or chart to bring up specific formatting options.

Adding titles and labels

All types of graph and chart should have a title and labels.

1 Click the box surrounding the chart or graph.

2 Click the + that appears in the top right corner.

3 Select the 'Chart Element' you want to add or delete.

4 Change any standard text that appears when the titles or labels are added.

Moving a chart

To move a chart around the page, click on an edge and drag it.

You could be asked to move it to a new sheet.

1 Right-click a blank part of the chart box.

2 Select 'Move Chart...' from the menu.

3 Choose 'New sheet' and click 'OK'.

A new sheet will be made with the title 'Chart1'. You can choose it in the tabs at the bottom.

Editing titles and labels

Titles and labels must stand out and be easy-to-read. Clicking the text box once allows you to resize or move the text. Double-clicking it allows you to add, change and delete text.

Make sure the titles and labels are:

- relevant
- spelled correctly
- not complete sentences (no full stops)
- completely visible.

Getting it right

If you are asked to move a chart onto a new sheet, **do not** cut and paste. Make sure you use the 'Move Chart' option.

You can make sure headings and labels are clear by increasing their size (16 pt) and making them bold.

Now try this

- Open the file **StaffListPG54L1** and resave it with a new name.
- Create a suitable chart to display all the salaries by surname.
- Give your chart an appropriate title.
- Move it to a new sheet and format it so it is clear and easy-to-read.

Putting it into practice

In the test, you will need to produce a graph or chart from data. Make sure you:

✓ select the correct data

✓ choose the most appropriate type of graph of chart

✓ format the graph or chart so that it is clear and easy to understand.

 Open the file BrickSuppliesPG55L1

Create a chart to display a breakdown of the total cost of the bricks by type of brick.

The chart must:

- be clearly labelled
- be easy to understand
- have an appropriate title
- be saved on a separate worksheet within your spreadsheet.

 If you're asked to compare parts of a whole, use a pie chart. In this question, the whole is the total cost of the bricks.

Make sure your chart includes everything that the question asks for. You can use the bullet points as a checklist.

Use formatting to make sure the different segments of your chart are easy-to-read and understand, especially if you are printing in black and white.

Evidence

A printout of your chart, and your spreadsheet saved in your test folder.

(4 marks)

 Open the file TravelCostsPG55L1

The spreadsheet shows costs that a travel agent has found for a customer who wants to book a holiday.

Create a chart to compare the total cost for the five destinations, excluding extras such as drinks and snacks.

The chart must:

- be clearly labelled
- be easy to understand
- have an appropriate title
- be saved on a separate worksheet within your spreadsheet.

 If you're asked to compare different groups or options, use a bar chart.

Remember to add labels to both axes. Include any units (such as pounds) in the label.

Move your chart to a new sheet using the correct method. Don't copy and paste.

Evidence

A printout of your chart, and your spreadsheet saved in your test folder.

(4 marks)

Understanding presentations

In the test, you could be asked to produce a slide show presentation.
This guide will help you to revise how to produce an effective slide show presentation using Microsoft® PowerPoint 2013.

Slide show presentations

Microsoft® PowerPoint allows you to create and display slide show presentations, which can consist of any number of slides. You can add text, images, videos, animations and sounds to your slide show to inform and entertain your audience.

Displaying presentations

You can choose to display one slide at a time, manually clicking through the slides while you talk. Or, you can make the slide show run automatically, like the ones you find on websites or in the receptions of hotels, colleges and other businesses.

Getting it right

To produce a clear, appealing presentation in the test, you should include:

✓ suitable headings

✓ bullet points showing key information

✓ any images asked for, and no others

✓ videos and sound files if asked to

✓ a suitable font, text size and colour scheme.

The main parts of a presentation

 The **first slide** should contain:

- the main title – often the name of the company or organisation, or the subject of the talk

- a subtitle – such as the name of the presenter, or an interesting phrase to catch the audience's attention.

Dinglewood Motors
Motoring specialist

Dinglewood Motors
Latest promotion!

 The **main slides** should contain:

- the key information (with a new slide for each of the main points).

 The **final slide** should contain:

- thanks to your audience

- contact details

- an invitation for questions

- any final thoughts you want to leave your audience with.

Dinglewood Motors
Motoring specialist

Any questions?

Contact: Lorrayn Smith-Carterson
Telephone: 01632 431298
Email: lscarterson@dinglewood.bus.org

Slides need to be visible from a distance and may not be displayed for long, so keep your points clear and concise.

Go to page 33 for information on audience and purpose.

Now try this

- Open the file **PaintersPG56L1**

- Make a list of things that could be improved to make the presentation more effective.

Creating a presentation

If you are asked to produce a slide show presentation in the test, you will be given:

- a Microsoft® Notepad file containing text
- a selection of images.

You could also be given a video or sound file.

Creating a new presentation

1 Find the application by typing 'powerpoint' in the Search box. Double-click the icon.

2 Choose 'Blank Presentation'.

3 Save your presentation straightaway with a suitable name in the correct folder.

Click to add title

Click to add subtitle

Inserting slides

Look at the slide numbers in the Microsoft® Notepad file to work out how many slides you need in your presentation. You will already have the title page, but you'll need to add the other pages. To add a new slide:

1 Click the 'Insert' tab and choose 'New slide'.

2 Choose the 'Two Content' layout.

Reordering slides

If you need to rearrange the order of the slides, you can simply drag them up or down in the 'slides pane'. To delete a slide, click on it in the 'slides pane' and press the Delete key on your keyboard.

Adding text to slides

Copy and paste each piece of text carefully from the Microsoft® Notepad file to the appropriate slide. Start with the title and subtitle on the first slide, and continue until the final slide.

When all the text is in place, you should think about using text formatting and add the images you're asked to include, on relevant slides.

Go to page 58 to revise formatting.

 Don't include the words 'Title slide' or the slide numbers in your presentation – they are only there to help you.

Getting it right

Make sure you copy across all of the text supplied. Maximise the Microsoft® Notepad window so you can see everything.

Now try this

- Open the file **PromotionPG57L1**
- Use the text to create a slide show presentation that will run in the car showroom where you work. There is no need to add any formatting or images just yet.

Formatting and design

In the test, you will need to show that you can use formatting, such as bold, italics, underline and font colour to enhance the way your presentation looks.

Formatting text

You can make titles and subtitles bold, large and different colours to make them stand out. Remember, the title should be larger than the subtitle.

You can use bullet points to break up the key information into smaller sections. Make sure bulleted text is large enough to be read from a distance – size 26 is a suitable size.

Golden rule

As in word-processing tasks, you should not use WordArt. Avoid using all capital letters (even for titles) as they can be difficult to read from a distance.

Formatting colour

You can add colourful borders and backgrounds to your slide show to make it look more eye-catching.

Make sure the colour of your text and background are suitable - choose either a light text on a dark background or a dark text on a light background.

Dinglewood Motors

Motoring specialist

Any questions?

Contact: Lorrayn Smith-Carterson
Telephone: 01632 431298
Email: lscarterson@dinglewood.bus.org

Consistent formatting

You should keep formatting consistent through your slide show. This means picking a colour scheme and using the same size text and style throughout.

Dinglewood Motors

Motoring specialist

This week only

- 10% discount on showroom prices
- Free services for 2 years
- Free tyre checks every 6 months

Now try this

- Open the file **PromotionPG58L1**
- Apply suitable formatting, drawing attention to key information.
- Save it with a new file name.
  There's no need to add any images just yet.

Adding images

You can add images to your presentation to help to explain your ideas and to make your presentation look eye-catching. You could be given a selection of images to include in your slide show or you may be asked to use one you've saved in your Responses document.

Inserting images

In the test you could be given a folder of images to choose from.

Inserting images in Microsoft® PowerPoint works in exactly the same way as it does in Microsoft® Word. The same goes for copying, resizing, cropping and drawing shapes.

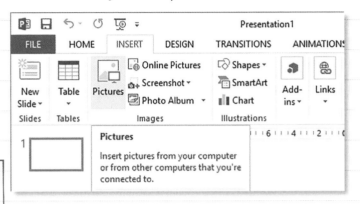

Choosing the right images

Read the task to work out how many images you need to insert and where you need to insert them. Don't be tempted to add more images than you are asked to.

The image you put on each slide should relate to the text. You could be given an image in the test that isn't relevant, so you need to choose carefully.

Go to page 31 to revise inserting and editing images.

Placing images

Choosing the 'Two Content' layout in Microsoft® PowerPoint allows you to easily place an image on one side of the slide, alongside the text.

1 Select the slide you want to add the image to.

2 Click the 'Insert' tab, then add an image, clipart or shape.

Alternatively, you can drag the image file from the folder and drop it into the slide.

Remember, you're not allowed to go on the internet in this part of the test, so don't use the 'Online Pictures' option.

Inserting logos

You could be asked to insert a logo on every slide.

1 Insert or copy the logo on to one slide.

2 Resize the logo and drag it into a suitable position. Logos should be smaller than any other image and they are normally placed in the corner.

3 Right-click to copy the logo.

4 Paste it into the same area on all of the other slides.

Now try this

- Open the file **PromotionPG59L1**
- Look in the folder **ImagesPG59L1** for the Dinglewood Motors logo.
- Position the logo appropriately on each slide.
- Position one suitable image on each of slides 2–4.
- Save the file with a suitable name.

Adding sound and video

In the test, you could be asked to insert an audio (sound) file or video clip into your presentation.

Inserting an audio file

In the test, you could be given an audio file to include in your presentation.

1 Go to the slide where you want to add the audio file. Go to the 'Insert' tab, then click 'Audio' and choose 'Audio on My PC'.

2 You will be supplied with an audio file with the image files. Select the audio file in the folder. Double-click the file to insert it.

3 A speaker icon will appear on the slide. You can resize and move this icon in the same way as an image.

Sound files will usually end in .mp3, .wav or .wma.
Video files will usually end in .mp4, .avi, .mov or .mpg.

Inserting a video file

In the test, you could be given a video file to include in your presentation.

1 Go to the slide where you want to add the video file. Go to the 'Insert' tab, then click 'Video' and choose 'Video on my PC'.

2 You will be supplied with a video file with the image files. Select the video file in the folder. Double-click the file to insert it.

3 If the slide is formatted as a 'Two Content' layout, the video will appear on one side. On a blank slide template, it will fill the whole slide. You can make a video appear smaller by clicking and dragging the corners, in the same way you would resize an image.

To remove a video or audio file from a slide, click the video or the speaker icon and press 'delete' on your keyboard. This doesn't delete the video file from the computer, it just removes it from the slide show.

Now try this

- Open the file **RelaxationPG60L1**
- Insert the sound file **BabblingBrook**
- Move the icon to a suitable position.
- Insert the video **Meadows** on a new blank slide.
- Save the file with a suitable name.

Checking and final touches

When you have completed the task, you should spend some time checking your presentation from start to finish.

Things to check

 Text

Read the text in your slide show carefully.

- Have you copied across all the text correctly?
- Does every page have a title?
- Have you corrected any spelling mistakes?
- Does the information you've added (e.g. from your internet search or spreadsheet) make sense?
- Have you accidentally left in any guidance from the text file, such as 'Title' or 'Slide 2'?

> Remember to maximise the Microsoft® Notepad window to check you have included all the text.

 **Images**

Look back at the task instructions about images and logos.

- Have you inserted the correct number of images?
- Are the images placed with the text that they're related to?
- Have you included a logo on every page (if needed)?
- Have you distorted any of the images when you resized them?

> Go to page 59 to revise adding images and logos.

 Formatting

Check that the formatting you have used is consistent throughout your slide show presentation.

- Is the bulleted text large enough to read from a distance (size 24 or larger)?
- Are the main title, subtitle and slide titles larger than the bullet text? Are they bold?
- Is there a good contrast between the font colour and any background colour?
- Do you have a colour scheme that links every slide?

④ Adding headers and footers

In the test, you will be asked to include your name, candidate number and centre number in the footer of documents you edit or produce.

1 Click the 'Insert' tab, then select 'Header and Footer'.

2 Tick the box next to 'Footer' and type your details in the box beneath.

3 Click 'Apply to All'. The details will then appear at the bottom of every slide, including any new ones you add.

Now try this

A junior employee has attempted to produce a short presentation for the owner of Musical Painters to use at a staff meeting.

- Open the file **PlanningPG61L1**
- Format the presentation so that it is suitable for the purpose and audience.
- Make sure all slides feature the company logo.
- Save the file with a suitable name.

Slide show and print options

In the test, you won't be showing your presentation to an audience, but you need to be able to see what it would look like. You could be asked to print your slides, so make sure you are familiar with all of the options.

Printing slides

If you are asked to print slides, go to the 'Home' tab, click 'File' and choose 'Print'.

If you choose 'Print All Slides', each slide will print out full size on a separate sheet.

Alternatively, you can click the drop-down menu and choose to print just the slide you're looking at, or specific ones.

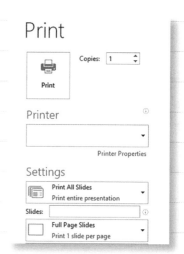

Printing hand-outs

In the test, you could be given a scenario where you need to print hand-outs for an audience. Handouts like the one on the right usually display several slides on each page.

Click the drop-down menu next to 'Full Page Slides' to see the options. Some of them will provide space for notes next to the slides.

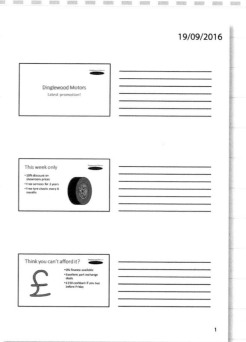

Playing a slide show

To play your slide show, click the 'Slide show' tab.

You can run your show from the beginning or from whichever slide you have on screen.

After the last slide, you'll see a black screen: click to return to the normal view.

Now try this

Your boss has asked you to produce printed hand-outs with your presentation. What steps would you follow to produce a hand-out with four slides per page?

Putting it into practice

You could be asked to create a clear and consistent presentation in the test. You need to use the text file and images provided to help you to produce an effective presentation in Microsoft® PowerPoint.

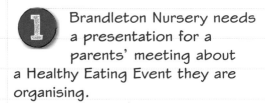 **1** Brandleton Nursery needs a presentation for a parents' meeting about a Healthy Eating Event they are organising.

 Use text formatting, such as bold and bullet points, to make your presentation easy-to-read.

The presentation must:

- contain 5 slides
- be clear and easy-to-read
- have a consistent format
- be fit for purpose and audience.

 The audience is parents of nursery children. Make sure you choose appropriate images and language for an adult audience.

It must include:

- **relevant** text from **EventPG63L1**
- the **correct logo** from **ImagesPG63L1** on each slide
- the sound file **CarrotPeelerL1** on Slide 2
- one appropriate image on each of slides 2–4, selected from **ImagesPG63L1**
- the name of the company you found in **Task 1**.

Choose the logo image carefully and make sure it appears in every slide.

 As Task 1 is not part of this practice exercise, the information you need is: **Brandleton Bistro.**

Evidence

A copy of your presentation saved in a new folder on your desktop.

(4 marks)

Answers

Getting started

1. Preparing for your test

1. 5

2. Name, candidate number and centre number

2. Starting up and shutting down

1. That your work is saved; that nobody else is logged on

2. Check that Caps Lock isn't on

3. Hardware

Touch screens (you can enter data and view it); headsets with microphone and earphones (you can speak into them and hear through them)

4. Software

To find the prices of items for the sweet stall, I'll open a **web browser**, such as Microsoft® Edge and use a search engine. I will put the costs into a **spreadsheet** using Microsoft® **Excel** and then make a pie **chart** showing a breakdown of the costs. Next, I have to make a poster, so I'll use Microsoft® **Word** which is a **word processing** application. I will email the chart and the poster to my manager using Microsoft® **Outlook**. Finally, I will make a slideshow presentation for the next board meeting using Microsoft® **PowerPoint**.

5. Windows®

- Type 'Calculator' in the Search box and click the application to open it.
- Click the minus button to minimise the window.
- To restore it, click the application icon on the taskbar.
- To close it, click the cross.

6. Problem solving

Using offline help, you should have found a list of links. Clicking 'More about Font Colour' will take you to instructions to help you.

7. Health and safety

Give your friend the following advice:

- make sure you wear your glasses if you need them.
- don't sit too close to the screen – about 50–80 cm away is good.
- make sure there aren't reflections on the screen – turn it around a bit if there are, and adjust the brightness if you need to.
- take frequent breaks from staring at the screen.

8. Settings and accessibility

1. She could reverse the way the mouse buttons work

2. The Magnifier and the Narrator

9. Files and folders

There is no model answer for this task. Make sure you are confident with this topic. Ask your teacher for help if you need additional support.

10. Saving and printing

There is no model answer for this task. Make sure you are confident with this topic. Ask your teacher for help if you need additional support.

11. Storing and backing-up

1. Any one of: USB memory stick; external hard drive; CD; DVD; Blu-Ray(tm).

2. Any two of:
- your laptop could be lost or stolen
- malware could damage your files
- hackers could damage your files
- your computer could get damaged or develop a fault.

12. Screen shots

There is no model answer for this task. Make sure you are confident with this topic. Ask your teacher for help, if you need additional support.

13. Keeping your information safe

(a) nursery ✏ too easy to guess and only contains letters

(b) nUr5Ery£ 🔑 numbers are used for letters, contains a mix of capital and small letters, and the £ sign makes it even more difficult to guess

(c) 12345678 ✏ too easy to guess and only contains numbers

(d) Malcolm ✏ too short, easy to guess and only contains letters

14. Putting it into practice

1. B, **because it uses:**
- a mixture of upper and lower case letters
- numbers in place of some of the letters
- a symbol

2. • Install antivirus software and keep it updated.
- Avoid getting viruses by not clicking on links in emails from people I don't know or using illegal download sites.

3. Answers could include any two of each:
Input devices: keyboard, microphone, mouse
Output devices: screen, speakers, monitor
There are other valid answers.

4. Any one of: Narrator, Magnifier, High Contrast theme, Speech Recognition

5. Answers could include any two of:
- wear glasses if you are supposed to
- sit with your back straight, lower back supported and shoulders relaxed
- keep your feet flat on the floor or on a foot rest
- check that the screen is 50–80 cm away.

6. Answers could include:
- your computer could be lost or stolen
- malware could damage or delete your files
- your computer could be damaged or develop a fault

The internet

15. internet

1. The **web** is the name for a collection of **websites** that can be accessed via the **internet**. Websites are made up of **webpages**.

2. There's no dot after www

16. Navigating a website

There is no model answer for this task. Make sure you are confident with this topic. Ask your teacher for help, if you need additional support.

17. Searching and saving

Open the file **AnswerPG17L1** to compare your work with the model answer.

The name of the castle is:

Clitheroe

The postcode of the museum is:

BB7 1BA

The keywords are: **castle Ribble Valley**

18. Evaluating information

B, because it will give you a selection of unbiased opinions.

19. Staying legal

1. Using someone's written work, image, music, video or software without permission
2. Public domain images

20. Putting it into practice

1. Open file **AnswerPG20L1** to compare your work with the model answer.
2. Information could be out of date, unreliable or biased.

Email

21. What is email?

Answers could include: Advantages:
- she can email lots of people at the same time
- she can keep a record of what has been said

Disadvantages:
- they might not read all their emails
- she won't know whether her email was received.

22. Sending and receiving emails

Open file **AnswerPG22L1** to compare your work with the model answer.

23. Email attachments

Open the file **AnswerPG23L1** to compare your work with the model answer.

24. Getting emails right

There is no model answer for this task. Make sure you are confident with this topic. Ask your teacher for help, if you need additional support.

25. Safe and savvy online

Your bank will never email you asking for your online banking login details. You should ignore the email and contact you bank.

26. Putting it into practice

Open the file **AnswerPG26L1** to compare your work with the model answer.

Word processing

27. Entering text

Open the file **AnswerPG27L1** to compare your work with the model answer.

28. Formatting text

Open the file **AnswerPG28L1** to compare your work with the model answer.

29. Page layout

Open the file **AnswerPG29L1** to compare your work with the model answer.

30. Using tables

Open the file **AnswerPG30L1** to compare your work with the model answer.

31. Using images

Open the file **AnswerPG31L1** to compare your work with the model answer.

32. Using text boxes and shapes

Open the file **AnswerPG32L1** to compare your work with the model answer.

33. Audience and purpose

1. Answers could include:
   - choose plain sans serif fonts
   - use mainly black and white, with a few colours if suitable
   - use tables to display information clearly
2. Answers could include:
   - don't use too many colours
   - make sure fonts are easy to read

34. Posters and adverts

1. Answers could include:
   - Choose plain sans serif fonts.
   - Use mainly black and white, with few colours if suitable.
   - Use tables to display information clearly.
2. Answers could include:
   - Don't use too many colours.
   - Make sure fonts are easy to read.

35. Newsletters, leaflets and flyers

Open the file **AnswerPG35L1** to compare your work with the model answer.

36. Letters and business documents

Open the file **AnswerPG36L1** to compare your work with the model answer.

37. Checking your work

Open the file **AnswerPG37L1** to compare your work with the model answer.

38. Putting it into practice

Open the file **AnswerPG38L1** to compare your work with the model answer.

Spreadsheets?

39. What are spreadsheets?

1. £615.43

2. A5

40. Entering and changing data

Open the file **AnswerPG40L1** to compare your work with the model answer.

41. Rows and columns

Open the file **AnswerPG41L1** to compare your work with the model answer.

42. Formatting data

Open the file **AnswerPG42L1** to compare your work with the model answer.

43. Using simple formulas

Open the file **AnswerPG43L1** to compare your work with the model answer.

44. SUM, MIN and MAX

Open the file **AnswerPG44L1** to compare your work with the model answer.

45. Averages

Open the file **AnswerPG45L1** to compare your work with the model answer.

46. Sorting and filtering

Open the file **AnswerPG46L1** to compare your work with the model answer.

47. Viewing and printing formulas

Open the file **AnswerPG47L1** to compare your work with the model answer.

48. Putting it into practice

Open the file **AnswerPG48L1** to compare your spreadsheet with the model answer.

Charts and graphs

49. Types of charts and graphs

(a) A line graph – the temperature is changing over time.

(b) A column or bar chart – showing the share of a total wouldn't be meaningful.

(c) A pie chart – it would be easy to see what fraction of the day was spent on different activities.

50. Selecting data for a chart

Open the file **AnswerPG50L1** to compare your spreadsheet with the model answer.

51. Pie charts

Open the file **AnswerPG51L1** and click **Chart1** to compare your chart with the model answer.

52. Column and bar charts

Open the file **AnswerPG52L1** and click **Chart2** and **Chart3** to compare your charts with the model answers.

53. Line graphs

Open the file **AnswerPG53L1** and click **Chart1** to compare your chart with the model answer.

54. Formatting charts and graphs

Open the file **AnswerPG54L1** and look at **Chart1** and **Chart2** to compare your work with the model answers. Either a column chart or a bar chart would be acceptable.

55. Putting it into practice

1. Open the file **Answer1PG55L1** and click **Chart1** to compare your work with the model answer.

2. Open the file **Answer2PG55L1** and click **Chart 1** to compare your work with the model answer

Presentations

56. Understanding presentations

Answers could include: could include:

- the font on the title slide is much too small.
- the logo is too large and hides part of the title.
- slide 2 has far too much information on it; it's very cluttered.
- the fonts on Slide 2 are too small.
- the content of Slide 2 could not be seen from a distance.
- the information on Slide 2 is a flyer and should have been produced in word-processing software.
- the background of Slide 2 is too dark and makes the text hard to read.
- slide 3 does not provide any information. There should be contact details or some other instruction, or thanks for help.

57. Creating a presentation

Open the file **AnswerPG57L1** to compare your presentation with the model answer.

58. Formatting and design

Open the file **AnswerPG58L1** to compare your presentation with the model answer.

59. Adding images

Open the file **AnswerPG59L1** to compare your presentation with the model answer.

60. Adding sound and video

Open the file **AnswerPG60L1** to compare your presentation with the model answer.

61. Checking and final touches

Open the file **AnswerPG61L1** to compare your presentation with the model answer.

62. Slide show and print options

If you had difficulty with these tasks, ask your teacher for additional help with these topics. The invigilator will not be able to help you in the test.

63. Putting it into practice

Open the file **AnswerPG63L1** to compare your presentation with the model answer.

Notes

Notes

Notes

Published by Pearson Education Limited, 80 Strand, London, WC2R 0RL.

www.pearsonschoolsandfecolleges.co.uk

Copies of official specifications for all Edexcel qualifications may be found on the website: www.edexcel.com

Text © Pearson Education Limited 2016
Edited, typeset and produced by Elektra Media Ltd
Original illustrations © Pearson Education Limited 2016
Illustrated by Elektra Media Ltd
Cover illustration by Miriam Sturdee

The right of Alison Trimble to be identified as author of this work has been asserted by her in accordance with the Copyright, Designs and Patents Act 1988.

First published 2016

19 18 17 16
10 9 8 7 6 5 4 3 2 1

British Library Cataloguing in Publication Data
A catalogue record for this book is available from the British Library

ISBN 978 1 292 14592 1

Printed in Slovakia by Neografia

Acknowledgements
The author and publisher would like to thank the following individuals and organisations for permission to reproduce photographs:
(Key: c-centre;)

Shutterstock.com: Andreas G. Karelias 35c,

All other images © Pearson Education

MICROSOFT AND/OR ITS RESPECTIVE SUPPLIERS MAKE NO REPRESENTATIONS ABOUT THE SUITABILITY OF THE INFORMATION CONTAINED IN THE DOCUMENTS AND RELATED GRAPHICS PUBLISHED AS PART OF THE SERVICES FOR ANY PURPOSE. ALL SUCH DOCUMENTS AND RELATED GRAPHICS ARE PROVIDED "AS IS" WITHOUT WARRANTY OF ANY KIND. MICROSOFT AND/OR ITS RESPECTIVE SUPPLIERS HEREBY DISCLAIM ALL WARRANTIES AND CONDITIONS WITH REGARD TO THIS INFORMATION, INCLUDING ALL WARRANTIES AND CONDITIONS OF MERCHANTABILITY, WHETHER EXPRESS, IMPLIED OR STATUTORY, FITNESS FOR A PARTICULAR PURPOSE, TITLE AND NON-INFRINGEMENT. IN NO EVENT SHALL MICROSOFT AND/OR ITS RESPECTIVE SUPPLIERS BE LIABLE FOR ANY SPECIAL, INDIRECT OR CONSEQUENTIAL DAMAGES OR ANY DAMAGES WHATSOEVER RESULTING FROM LOSS OF USE, DATA OR PROFITS, WHETHER IN AN ACTION OF CONTRACT, NEGLIGENCE OR OTHER TORTIOUS ACTION, ARISING OUT OF OR IN CONNECTION WITH THE USE OR PERFORMANCE OF INFORMATION AVAILABLE FROM THE SERVICES.
THE DOCUMENTS AND RELATED GRAPHICS CONTAINED HEREIN COULD INCLUDE TECHNICAL INACCURACIES OR TYPOGRAPHICAL ERRORS. CHANGES ARE PERIODICALLY ADDED TO THE INFORMATION HEREIN. MICROSOFT AND/OR ITS RESPECTIVE SUPPLIERS MAY MAKE IMPROVEMENTS AND/OR CHANGES IN THE PRODUCT(S) AND/OR THE PROGRAM(S) DESCRIBED HEREIN AT ANY TIME. PARTIAL SCREEN SHOTS MAY BE VIEWED IN FULL WITHIN THE SOFTWARE VERSION SPECIFIED. MICROSOFT® WINDOWS®, MICROSOFT OFFICE®, MICROSOFT® WORD, MICROSOFT® EXCEL, MICROSOFT® POWERPOINT, MICROSOFT® BING, MICROSOFT® NOTEPAD, MICROSOFT® OUTLOOK, MICROSOFT® EDGE AND MICROSOFT® PUBLISHER ARE REGISTERED TRADEMARKS OF THE MICROSOFT CORPORATION IN THE U.S.A. AND OTHER COUNTRIES. THIS BOOK IS NOT SPONSORED OR ENDORSED BY OR AFFILIATED WITH THE MICROSOFT CORPORATION.

Google, Gmail and Chrome are trademarks of Google Inc.

Safari is a trademark of Apple Inc.

Firefox® is a registered trademark of the Mozilla Foundation.

A note from the publisher
In order to ensure that this resource offers high-quality support for the associated Pearson qualification, it has been through a review process by the awarding body. This process confirms that this resource fully covers the teaching and learning content of the specification or part of a specification at which it is aimed. It also confirms that it demonstrates an appropriate balance between the development of subject skills, knowledge and understanding, in addition to preparation for assessment.

Endorsement does not cover any guidance on assessment activities or processes (e.g. practice questions or advice on how to answer assessment questions), included in the resource nor does it prescribe any particular approach to the teaching or delivery of a related course.

While the publishers have made every attempt to ensure that advice on the qualification and its assessment is accurate, the official specification and associated assessment guidance materials are the only authoritative source of information and should always be referred to for definitive guidance.

Pearson examiners have not contributed to any sections in this resource relevant to examination papers for which they have responsibility.

Examiners will not use endorsed resources as a source of material for any assessment set by Pearson. Endorsement of a resource does not mean that the resource is required to achieve this Pearson qualification, nor does it mean that it is the only suitable material available to support the qualification, and any resource lists produced by the awarding body shall include this and other appropriate resources.